Warman's
MODERNISM
Furniture & Accessories

Published by

krause publications
A subsidiary of F+W Media, Inc.

700 East State Street • Iola, WI 54990-0001
715-445-2214 • 888-457-2873
www.krausebooks.com

Our toll-free number to place an order or obtain
a free catalog is (800) 258-0929.

Cover: Amy Lau Design for Sollo Rago Modern Auctions Designer Vignettes,
Photography by WynnPhoto.com.

Library of Congress Control Number: 2008937694

ISBN-13: 978-089689-969-8
ISBN-10: 0-89689-969-1

Designed by Katrina Newby
Edited by Mark Moran

Printed in China

Warman's

MODERNISM
Furniture & Accessories

IDENTIFICATION AND PRICE GUIDE

Noah Fleisher

contents

Charles and Ray Eames, 670/671 lounge chair and ottoman, chair
33" x 35" x 32", ottoman 26.5" x 21" x 17.5". **$1,500**

modernism
The genius of Post-Industrial Design

Welcome to *Warman's Modernism Furniture & Accessories*. This represents the culmination of a tremendous amount of work on behalf of myself and the editors, designers and staff of Krause Publications. We've all watched the market over the past few years and all feel that this is a price guide whose time has definitely come, and if you're reading this book right now, then you probably agree.

For the purposes of this book we've chosen to limit our scope to between 1945 and 1985, give or take a decade or two on either side where necessary. It is, however, wrong to suggest there is not much great Modernism pre-1930 or post-2000. "Modernism" didn't just one day emerge, say Jan. 1, 1950, fully realized, from the mind of its remote creators.

It is the stuff of the 1933 Chicago World's Fair "Century of Progress," the boundless optimism of post-World War II America, the sleek comic lines and manic music of Tex Avery's MGM 1949 "House of Tomorrow" cartoons, and the ever-present acres of the suburban ranch house that subsequently spread endlessly across the nation.

That form, those colors, the unbridled enthusiasm and audacious hope represented therein … It all hearkens back to post-War 1950s America, when the West was ready to embrace the new realities of easy living and convenience.

Lino Sabattini, candlesticks with spiral arms, pair, 11.5"..... **$750**

The fact is that Modernism has never gone out of style. Its reach into the present day is as deep as its roots in the past. Just as it can be seen and felt ubiquitously in the mass media of today – on film, television, in magazines and department stores – it can be traced to the mid-1800s post-Empire non-conformity of the Biedermeier Movement, the turn of the 20th century anti-Victorianism of the Vienna Secessionists, the radical reductionism of Frank Lloyd Wright and the revolutionary post-Depression thinking of Walter Gropius and the Bauhaus school in Germany. There is no end to the ways in which the movement of Modernism, its evolution and continuing influence, can be parsed. To that end, there is more than a little irony in the fact that, in the world of collecting, Modern has a retro connotation.

In today's economic climate, Modern is as close to a sure bet as collectors – experienced and neophyte alike – are going to get. From there, however, it's a game of names and taste. Do you gravitate to Scandinavian design? American? Chairs or tables? Loveseats or sofas? Art? Sculpture? Lighting?

Ask the experts where to put your money and energy when it comes to buying Modern and you'll invariably get two answers: Put your energy into what you love, and your money into the best that you can afford. What that means on an individual basis is as varied, however, as the Modern movement itself.

"The Modernists really changed the way the world looked," said John Sollo, a partner in Sollo Rago Auction of Lambertville, N.J. "What I personally love about Modernism is that the business, as with a lot of other areas of antiques, hasn't cut it off in some arbitrary way. We've said, 'Yeah, that's cool' to anything made from 1903 to 2003. That opens it up."

That openness is key, not only to the current success of Modernism as a philosophy of design, but also as an area of collecting. Sollo's partner in business, and one of the most recognizable names in the field, David Rago, takes Sollo's idea a little further by saying that Modernism is actually more about the names behind the design than the design itself, at least as far as buying goes. It's hard to disagree with that, as evidenced by the way that the listings in this book are broken down, form first followed by designer.

Gertrud and Otto Natzler, bowl, multi-hued blue glaze, 7" x 3" $2,000

"A decade ago people were buying up everything they could with the name Eames on it," Rago said, referring to Charles and Ray Eames, the husband-wife design team. "Today you can still get great deals on designs by modern masters. You just have to be informed about what you're doing. Go to major auctions and specialty Modernism shows. Talk to experts and learn as much as you can before you put money into it."

Richard Wright, the namesake of Wright20 in Chicago – a house whose Modern specialty auctions draw some of the very best examples of Modern design still available – echoes another idea that Rago put forth: that sometimes to be ahead of the curve you have to be behind it.

"There are bargains throughout the market starting at the turn of the century," said Wright. "Further, many early historical items are undervalued – or at least not hyped. Look for items out of fashion: 1930s Art Deco for example."

The word "bargain," as it refers to Modernism, must also be taken in context. A bargain can be $500, $5,000 or $50,000, depending on what, where and who you're buying. Again, it comes back to knowing your stuff. This can be accomplished by in-depth study, by association with reputable dealers and by taking your time and buying within your comfort zone.

Lisanne Dickson, Director of 1950s/Modern Design at Treadway-Toomey, goes into a little more depth on this, underscoring that a "bargain" price is relative, but certainly available.

"Classics of Modern design are undervalued and still fairly plentiful," she said. "After the 1999/2000 peak in prices, for example, designs by Charles and Ray Eames fell in value over the next seven years and have only started to firm within the last year. Prime examples can be had at fair prices, depending on how determined buyers are."

Dickson cites the current bargains in the U.S. market for big-name Scandinavian designers, and cautions entry-level buyers against going straight for the prime examples; they'll be priced out quickly.

"The closeness of an example to the original intentions of the designer is critically important," she said. "The earliest version of a design is most likely to represent the designer's true intention. Later modifications were likely made to enhance the bottom line, or ease production."

Those later designs are where an education can be had, collections formed and bargains found.

No discussion of Modern can be complete, however,

Jeff Koons, skateboard deck, blue, 31" x 8" **$1,000**

without examining its genesis and enduring influence. As discussed earlier, Modernism is everywhere in today's pop culture. Austere Scandinavian furniture dominates the television commercials that hawk hotels and mutual funds. Post-war American design ranges across sitcom set dressings to movie sets patterned after Frank Lloyd Wright houses and Hollywood Modernist classics set high in the hills.

What is *de rigueur* for any villain plotting to take over the world? A Bauhaus-inspired lair. No corporate headquarters is complete without "Modern" art on its walls, and chairs and tables straight out of the van der Rohe, Wormley, Knoll and Perriand catalogs. In the same breath, however, you have to look at the dorm rooms of college students and the apartments of young people whose living spaces are packed with the undeniably Modern mass-produced products of IKEA, Target, Design Within Reach and the like.

Along those lines, then, here's how Peter Loughrey, owner of Los Angeles Modern Auctions, puts it:

Paul Evans, welded steel ball table lamp with spherical glass shade, circa 1960, 25.5" x 12" **$4,750**

"Cheap rentals," he said simply. "You see a ton of print ads with Modern-designed items because rental of these things was relatively easy to come across. These are mass-produced pieces, and agencies could easily order up sets of five, 10 or 50 chairs for an ad or other marketing venture. Once these started popping up, there was no stopping it!"

This is an interesting theory, and there can be no denying that the post-World War II manufacturing techniques, and subsequent boom led to the widespread acceptance of plastic and bent plywood chairs along with low-sitting coffee tables, couches and recliners.

Wright takes this idea one step further, speaking of Modernism's appeal on an individual basis, despite its mass-production origins.

"The Modern aesthetic is the culture of our times," he said. "We live in a post-Modern world that freely borrows from all past styles. In addition, art and design have become signifiers to a large group of the upper-middle class. We are increasingly individually designing our world. Technology fuels this and the wide range of choices available."

"The modern aesthetic grew out of a perfect storm of post-war optimism, innovative materials and an incredible crop of designers," said Dickson. "The wide availability of the designs has made them accessible to the general public at reasonable prices."

On a more philosophic note, we can turn once more to Sollo, who posits that – even though Modern design has that "retro" feel – its time may have barely just arrived, if it's even come yet.

"I think that the people who designed the furniture were maybe ahead of society's ability to accept and understand what they were doing," he said. "It's taken people another 30 to 40 years to catch up to it, and that's what we're seeing now."

It is quite possible, taking Sollo's point to heart, that we are indeed living in the era when "Modernism" has finally come into its own, where it's finally understood as relevant across all levels of culture.

All of the experts consulted for this introduction put the bottom line for perspective buyers at almost the same place: find a dealer that you trust, go to specialty Modern auctions, sales and shows and ask as many questions as you possibly can. There is no such thing as a bad question when it comes to a "Modern" education.

Once you are well equipped with the proper knowledge of what you like and where to get it, there are tremendous deals to be had at whatever level you're

Isamu Noguchi/Herman Miller, rare "Rudder" stool, model no. IN-22, birch with two tubular steel legs, unmarked, 17" x 20.5". **$20,000**

buying. From $100 to $1,000 to $100,000, if you know unequivocally what you're after, then "Modern" is yours for the taking.

Throughout the pages of this book you will find brief descriptions of certain key designers in the Modern Movement. Some are amply represented in these pages and some only show up once or twice. In the case of the latter, their principle work may have come before or after the loosely defined years that this guide encompasses – otherwise we'd have an encyclopedia instead of a guide – or prices for the body of their work are readily available from a number of other sources.

These designers do not comprise a definitive list of Modernism. There are hundreds of great Modern designers, many of whom worked across categories – furniture, architecture, fine art, etc. – and many contributed to the work of other big names without ever seeking that glory for themselves. If you are already well versed in Modernism, then consider these just a brief refresher. You could most likely name a dozen more that should have been included. If, however, you are just beginning the awesome journey of discovery that Modernism represents, then consider these the low board before working up to the high-dive. These are the basics, the fundamentals. How far you go with them is up to you.

Word of Thanks

I would like to take this opportunity to thank the experts – John Sollo, David Rago, Lisanne Dickson, Richard Wright and Peter Loughrey – who gave their time and expertise to this essay and to this book. In particular, Sollo Rago Modern Auctions in Lambertville, N.J. and Treadway Galleries in Cincinnati. None of this would have been possible without their generous help.

I would also like to thank *Krause Publications* and its fine books division. Without publisher Dianne Wheeler and editorial director Paul Kennedy, this book would not have come to fruition. Nor would it have been possible without the expertise, hard work and guidance of editor Mark Moran, who has been a great ally and a good friend throughout this entire process, and will remain so a far beyond.

Last but not least, I would like to give final thanks, and my undying love, to my wife Lauren for her endless support and infinite patience through the late nights and long days it has taken to put this price guide together. Without her, and without our daughter Fiona Anne – who I also give a big thank you to – I would not have had the persistence to put this together.

Noah Fleisher is a copywriter at Heritage Auction Galleries in Dallas. He has written extensively for *Style Century Magazine;* its blog, *StyleWire,* as well as *Antique Trader Magazine, New England Antiques Journal* and the *Northeast Journal of Antiques and Art,* among others. This is his first book for Krause Publications.

George Nakashima, side table with English walnut free-edge top on American walnut tripod base, early 1960s, 21.5" x 29" x 21" **$14,000**

While not the most extensive expression of Modernism, beds and bedroom furniture still contain a number of true gems of design by some of the greatest names in the business, including Nelson, Rohde, Wegner, van der Rohe and Nakashima. Best of all, the examples you'll find at auction and in shops are generally affordable, quite stylish and a great addition to any collection.

beds, bedroom furniture, daybeds

$1,000 and under

Bedroom furniture, 1960s, headboard 54" x 1.75" x 36", dresser 20.5" x 18.25" x 42.5", mirror 29" x 41.25" **$50**

George Nelson, headboard and footboard; headboard 54" x 2" x 34.5", footboard 54" x 2" x 19.75" **$225**

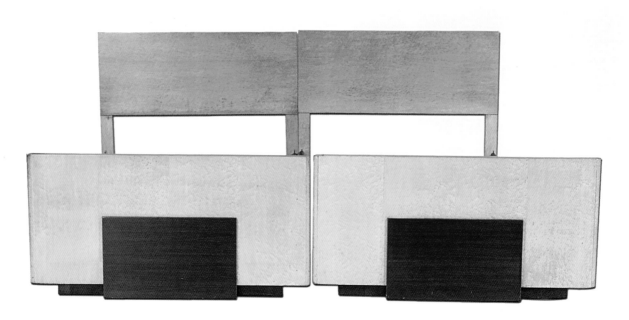

Gilbert Rohde/Herman Miller, twin beds in walnut and bird's eye maple veneer, each stenciled 3624, pair, each 33" x 41" x 79" **$500**

Peter Hvidt, daybed by France and Sons, 75" x 29.5" x 16" **$500**

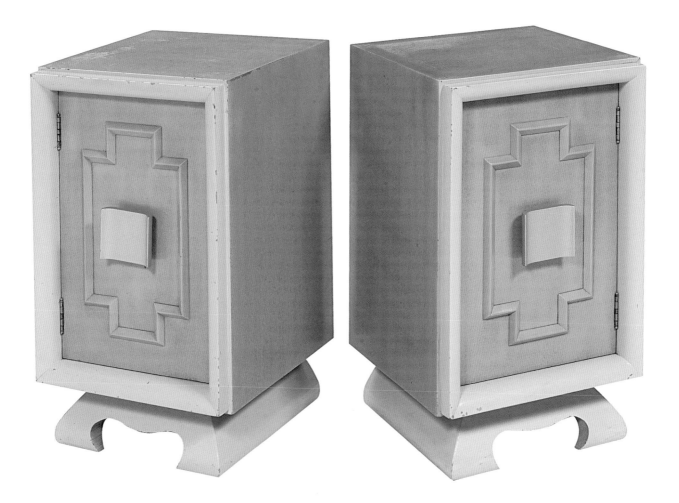

Kittinger, nightstands, each 16" x 15.75" x 26.5" . . . . **$550 pair**

Daybed, tufted seat cushion, off-white vinyl, 1960s, 76" x 30" x 22.5". **$700**

Gilbert Rohde, Mahogany full-size bed with storage headboard offering drawers, cabinets and shelving space, stenciled 4259, 40" x 88.5" x 82" **$900**

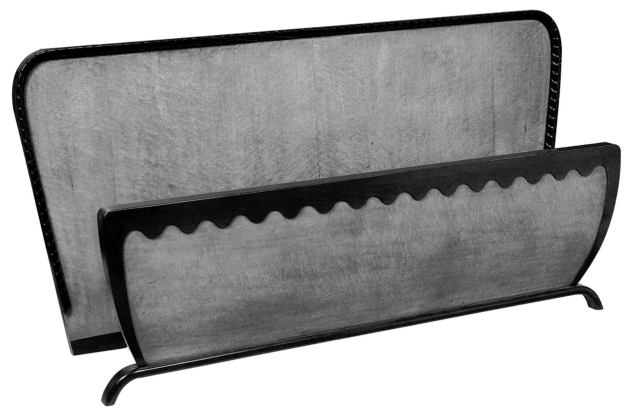

Bed, bird's eye maple, 1940s, Italy, headboard 88" x 41", opening for mattress approximately 64" **$1,000**

Ello, mirrored bedroom set consisting of a king-size platform bed with ultrasuede trim and illuminated top; a pair of three-door nightstands with illuminated tops; a small wardrobe; a six-drawer horizontal chest with two doors; and a pair of wall-hanging mirrors. Wardrobe 51.25" x 39.5" x 21", horizontal chest 30" x 75.25" x 21" . . . . **$1,000 set**

$1,000 to $3,000

Dresser and mirror, 1940s, Italy; cabinet 62" x 23" x 36", mirror 50" x 31", overall 67" **$1,200**

John Dunnigan, single bed in light wood, 38.25" x 43.5" x 80.75" **$1,200**

Bed, bird's eye maple veneer with two integrated single-door nightstands, and matching two-door wardrobe; bed: 23" x 106" x 93", interior width 61", wardrobe 76" x 39" x 18" **$1,250**

Willy Van Der Meeren, mahogany veneer wardrobe with sliding enameled metal doors concealing a clothes bar on one side, and fixed shelf on the other, 63" x 32" x 21" **$1,500**

George Nelson/Herman Miller, Thin Edge bed with caned headboard, 33" x 53" x 85" **$1,300**

Hans Wegner/Getama, twin bed with caned headboard, and integrated single-drawer nightstand, on tapering dowel legs. Nightstand has branded mark **$1,700**

Finn Juhl/Baker, full-size bed in teak and maple with slatted headboard, marked with Baker metal tag, 31.5" x 57" x 88" **$1,700**

Finn Juhl (1912-1989)

Finn Juhl was another of the wave of Danish designers that set the standard for sleek, thoughtful, organic Modern design in the 1950s. A graduate of the Copenhagen School of Arts and Crafts in 1924—the same school that produced Hans Wegner and Jens Risom – Juhl was probably the most exacting craftsman of all the Modern designers. It took a few years longer for fame to reach him, but made his contributions to Modernism carry great weight and lasting influence. He worked in small batches throughout the 1940s, contributing to Copenhagen Guild shows and focusing almost exclusively on creating the sound design fundamentals that would eventually make him one of Modernisms brightest stars.

It was his 1940 "Pelican" chair and the 1948 "Chieftain" chair that would really put Juhl on the map. He introduced the "floating back" concept in his chairs that would become so popular around the world, culminating in the delegate's chair he would design for the Trusteeship Council Chamber at the United Nations in New York City. Juhl would find his first and perhaps greatest commercial success in 1951 when he was commissioned by Baker Furniture in Michigan to create a series for the company's "younger" clientele. The line married Juhl's high standards of craftsmanship with affordable, modern production practices. Juhl's work also included influential glassware for Georg Jensen and refrigerators for General Electric.

Joaquin Tenreiro/Laubisch-Hirth, bedroom suite in exotic wood veneers with inlaid details, vanity and bench, pair of twin beds, chair and pair of two-drawer nightstands, Laubisch-Hirth decals to some; each bed 37" x 37" x 39", vanity 71" x 51" x 15" **$2,000**

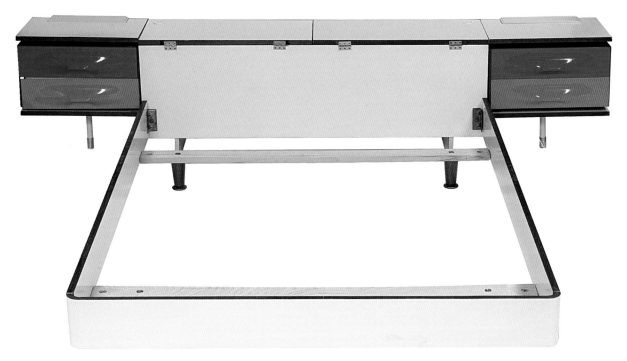

Raymond Loewy, DF-2000 full-size bed, 97" x 93" x 21" **$2,000**

Bruno Mathsson, queen size bed with mattress and orange slip cover (not shown), 22" x 62" x 79" **$2,000**

Charlotte Perriand, pine wardrobe with single sliding slatted door concealing four black tray drawers and storage compartments, on cylindrical black metal legs, 68" x 58" x 21" **$2,100**

Paul Evans, chrome patchwork bed, signed Paul Evans, 84" x 84" x 97". **$2,500**

Hannes Wettstein, Xen platform bed, 84.5" x 69" x 32" **$2,600**

George Nakashima, walnut storage headboard with double bed platform, 1959, 36" x 56" x 87" **$3,000**

Mies van der Rohe/Knoll, Barcelona daybed with tan leather upholstery to bolster and to tufted cushion, on wood frame with polished metal legs. Cushion has Art Metal/Knoll Associates tag, 24" x 73" x 3"... **$3,750**

Paul Laszlo, vanity in green lacquered finish, with pink embossed leather top, fitted with single drawer and lift-up mirror, the matching chair with pink ultra-suede cushions, circa 1952; vanity 29" x 37" x 24", chair 33" x 20" x 22".............................. **$4,000 set**

Jean Royere, daybed with tan cushion and bolster pillows on oak frame with inset cobalt glass panels, 32.5" x 65" x 32.75" **$4,000**

George Nakashima, walnut twin-size platform bed and headboard with sliding doors; bed 10" x 54" x 74.5", headboard 32" x 54" x 12" **$4,750**

George Nakashima, walnut double-twin headboard, 32" x 160" x 10" **$5,000**

Desks and credenzas are not the largest segment of Modernism, but they are among the most stylish, and the biggest names in the business all tried their hands at producing them. The relative lack of examples makes the best highly Sought after. Not to worry, though. Desks and credenzas by top designers like Wormley, Nelson and Baughman can still be had for under $1,000, and for just a few thousand dollars you can sometimes get lucky and bring home a superb example by names like Nakashima, Parisi or Ponti.

desks, credenzas

Also see Shelves, Storage.

$1,000 and under

Edward Wormley, desk with inset leather top, 43.75" x 24" x 30.5" **$75**

Richard Schultz, desk by Knoll, 1960s, 76" x 36" x 29.5" **$375**

Paul McCobb, desk and chair by Calvin, desk 55" x 26" x 31", chair 25" x 24" x 30". . . . . **$475 both**

George Nelson, L-unit desk by Herman Miller, 69" x 54" x 30"..**$650**

George Nelson, Action office desk, 65" x 32" x 40"..**$700**

Florence Knoll, single pedestal desk, 50" x 28" x 29" **$750**

George Nelson desk by Herman Miller, closed 40" x 24" x 29.75", open 58.25" **$800**

Desk, single-drawer, in wood veneer, one end faceted, the other curved, 29.5" x 45.5" x 22.5" **$1,000**

Warren McArthur, desk with ebonized wood top and drawers on aluminum frame, 28.5" x 44" x 24" **$1,000**

Edward Wormley/Dunbar, desk and file cabinet in ebonized wood and mahogany, with armchair, Dunbar metal and paper tags, desk 29" x 44" x 27", cabinet 23" x 15" x 25" . . . . **$1,000 set**

Birch credenza with burlwood veneer inlay, and interior shelves, on an ebonized platform base, Denmark, 32.5" x 77.75" x 21.5" **$1,250**

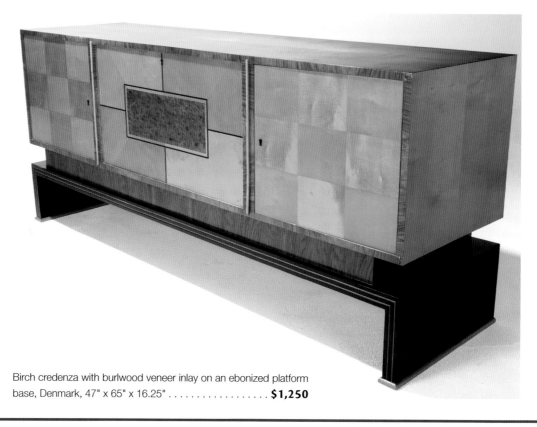

Birch credenza with burlwood veneer inlay on an ebonized platform base, Denmark, 47" x 65" x 16.25" **$1,250**

Milo Baughman/Thayer Coggin, campaign desk with white-lacquered wood top over chromed steel base, with chromed steel armchair upholstered in blue vinyl, Thayer Coggin tag to chair, table 28.75" x 54" x 24", chair 28" x 26.25" x 31.5" . . . . . **$1,500 both**

Steel mesh desk with accordion-folded steel drawer, France, 29.25" x 36" x 24.5" **$1,400**

Ernst Schwartz/Kagan Workshops, nine-drawer poplar desk with carved bands and laminate top, complete with inkwell, circa 1945, 30" x 65" x 25" **$1,500**

Gordon Bunshaft desk, 66" x 30" x 30" **$1,500**

Milo Baughman, executive desk, 78" x 36" x 29.5" **$1,600**

Finn Juhl /Baker, teak credenza with cane-front sliding doors enclosing drawers and shelf, Baker metal tag, 31" x 78" x 18" **$1,600**

Florence Knoll, large credenza, 108" x 18" x 23.5". **$1,600**

Raymond Loewy, DF2000 desk/cabinet, red molded plastic, 61" x 22.5" x 30.5" **$1,800**

Jean Prouve, oak and painted steel student desk and chair unit, with sliding iron inkwell, 25.5" x 23.5" x 32" **$1,900**

Florence Knoll/Knoll, eight-drawer walnut credenza on polished steel frame, 25.5" x 74.5" x 18" **$2,100**

Florence Knoll/Knoll, small rosewood credenza with white marble top on chrome base, 25.5" x 37.5" x 18" **$2,100**

Charles Eames/Herman Miller, ESU desk with birch top and colored panels in gray, black and beige, 29.75" x 60" x 28" **$2,400**

T.H. Robsjohn-Gibbings, ebonized walnut desk with brass ring pulls, along with side chair, desk 29.5" x 48" x 26", chair 34" x 20" x 24" . . . . **$2,500 both**

Edward Wormley/Dunbar, rosewood veneer L-shaped desk with oak tambour doors and interior, Dunbar brass tag, 53" x 60" x 82" **$2,600**

Hans Wegner/Ry Mobler, Oak credenza with two sliding doors enclosing four sliding trays and four adjustable shelves, with contrasing oak feet, stamped RY, 31" x 78.75" x 19.25" **$2,500**

Hans Wegner (1914-2007)

For the most part, Modern furniture could not necessarily be called playful, but that's exactly how many designs of Hans Wegner are described. Decidedly the most prolific designer of the cadre that emerged from the Copenhagen School of Arts & Crafts, Wegner was also possibly the most innovative of the Danish designers. As much as he strove for simplicity of design, Wegner also strove to make each individual piece of furniture stand on its own. This resulted in his focus on chairs, in particular. The result was work that became treasured and which routinely brings tens of thousands of dollars at auction. The good news for neophyte collectors is that there are still good examples of other Wegner furniture that can be had at auction or at shows for a few thousand dollars.

Wegner's first international sensation was his 1947 Peacock Chair, an inspired update of the traditional Windsor chair. He followed that with two more in 1949, a folding chair and the Shell chair. Both were innovative, as was his 1953 Valet chair, made for sitting as well as being crafted to hang up and/or store a man's suit, with a storage space beneath. Wegner's most iconic piece, however, is the Ox chair, which is a decidedly playful design that came with or without "horns." In the 1980s and 1990s, Wegner designed almost exclusively for PP Møbler, the firm that still produces most of his designs, and for whom he produced the Hoop chair in 1985, a highly desirable piece of late Modernism. Wegner worked actively until 1997, when he retired with more than 500 chair designs to his name.

Edward Wormley, kneehole desk, curved form, 58.25" x 30" x 29.25" **$3,250**

George Nelson/Herman Miller, swag-leg desk with two shallow drawers, 34.5" x 39" x 28.75" **$3,750**

George Nelson/Herman Miller, L-shaped CSS unit with desk includes: 12 drawers, two sliding door compartments and desktop in walnut veneer with dovetailed drawer fronts, desk complete with adjustable lamp and three-drawer filing cabinet, Nelson Miller circular metal tag, 98" x 96" x 65" **$4,000**

Edward Wormley/Dunbar, credenza with flame mahogany doors and ebony pulls, Dunbar brass tag, 35.25" x 65.25" x 18" **$4,000**

Jean Prouve, double-seat school desk with oak shelf and top, on green enameled metal base, 27" x 45" x 32" **$5,000**

Gilbert Rohde, Paldao desk, 56" x 28" x 29" **$4,500**

Carlo De Carli, rosewood desk with two book-matched veneer drawers on walnut and mahogany frame, 30.5" x 33.5" x 25.5". **$5,500**

Florence Knoll/Knoll, rosewood credenza with white marble top on chrome base, 25.75" x 74.5" x 17.75". **$6,500**

Paul Evans, sculpted bronze desk with plate glass top, 1972, 29.5"x 72" x 44.5" **$6,000**

George Nelson, home office desk with tan leather covering on sliding doors and writing surface, a lift-top storage compartment, and mesh Pendaflex file, 40.5" x 54" **$6,500**

George Nakashima, walnut single-pedestal, three-drawer desk with bitterroot pull, together with an armchair, desk 28" x 52" x 23.75", chair 28" x 23.5" x 17.75" . . . . **$7,000** **both**

Portenzac, single-pedestal desk covered in composite with six shaped drawers and steel leg, 30" x 63" x 26.75" **$6,500**

George Nakashima, walnut credenza, with two grass cloth-backed grilled doors enclosing two drawers, 28.5" x 22" x 20" **$7,500**

Florence Knoll, bleached maple credenza with two sliding grass-front doors enclosing interior shelves, on ebonized base, 32" x 72" x 16" **$10,000**

Ico Parisi, desk, 71" x 38.5" x 28.5". **$8,000**

$10,000 and up

Franco Albini, credenza in walnut veneer, parchment and chromed steel, the central compartment papered in red with glass doors and shelf, 38" x 106" x 21" **$11,000**

James Mont, desk in silver-leaf finish with carved Greek key bands and integrated jardinière, 28" x 66" x 28" **$17,000**

R & Y Augousti, green shagreen credenza with three drawers and two cabinet doors, 36" x 79" x 21" **$19,000**

Gio Ponti/Singer & Sons, two-drawer rosewood desk with tooled leather top and integrated magazine rack, circa 1950, 28.75" x 53.25" x 25.5" **$19,000**

George Nakashima, walnut double-pedestal desk with free-edge top, 29" x 85" x 31.5" **$21,000**

Paul Evans, deep-relief credenza with two bi-fold doors enclosing two interior shelves, welded mark, Paul Evans 68, 34.5" x 84" x 20.5" **$30,000**

Paul Evans, deep-relief credenza with two inset slate panels on top, and two bi-fold doors concealing interior shelves, 31" x 84" x 24" **$32,500**

George Nakashima, double-pedestal desk with rare Persian walnut free-edge top, circa 1969, 30" x 110" x 36". **$35,000**

lighting

desk and table lamps
$1,000 and under

It's only proper that lighting should be one of the major forms of Modern expression. All the major name designers and manufacturers produced lighting extensively through the middle 40 years of the 20th century. The shape and size varied as much as the artistic instincts of the designers themselves, and lights of all kinds continue to be a popular buy to this day.

Zahara Schatz, table lamp, Plexiglas, base 8.5" x 6" x 17.5", finial 31"....... **$125**

Table lamp, Laurel, 12" x 10" x 35"...................**$100**

Table lamp, flattened disk center, blue and brown, 1960s, Denmark, base 8.5", with shade 14"................... **$100**

Elio Martinelli, table lamp, model 643, 18" x 17" **$125**

Russell Wright, aluminum desk lamp, coiled base, 12" x 16.5" **$150**

George Cawardine, desk lamp, 36" as shown . . . . **$150**   Nelson, Bubble lamps, saucer form, two, 24.5" . . . . . . **$175 pair**

Table lamp, linen shade, 1950s, 6" x 6" x 14" **$275**

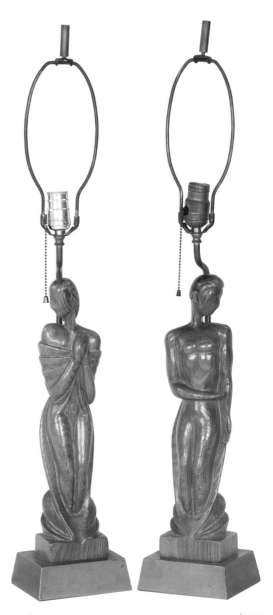

Edward Stasack, table lamps, 32.5" . . . . **$300 pair**

Table lamp, textured clear plastic panels, France, 11" x 5" x 13.5" **$225**

Koch & Lowy, table lamps, 14" x 22" . . . . **$200 pair**

Walter Von Nessen, table lamp, 29" x 24.5". **$350**

T Bönan, table lamp, 15.25" x 25.25" with shade, base is 15". . . .**$400**

Kaiser Idell, table lamp, 7" **$300**

Herman Miller, E-6310 table lamps, 15.25" x 26.5" . . . . **$300 pair**

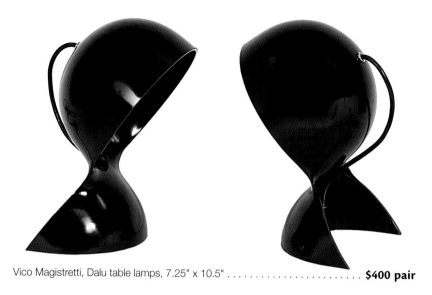

Vico Magistretti, Dalu table lamps, 7.25" x 10.5" . . . . **$400 pair**

Sergio Asti, table lamp, 16" x 41.5" **$450**

Greta von Nessen, "Anywhere" lamp, 12" x 12" x 14" **$475**

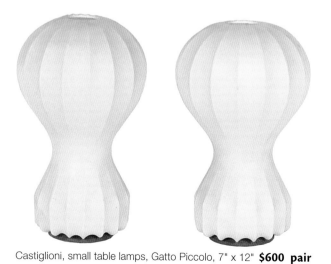

Castiglioni, small table lamps, Gatto Piccolo, 7" x 12" **$600 pair**

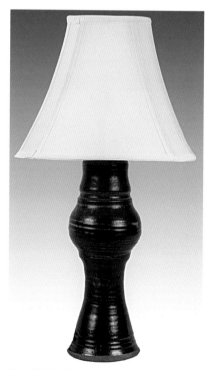

Frans Wildenhain, pottery table lamp, brown glaze, 6" x 16" **$500**

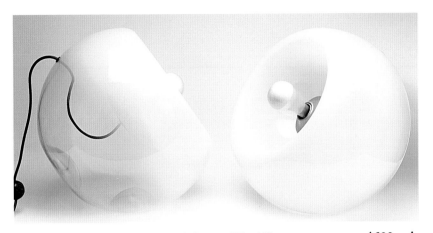

Eleonora Peduzzi-Riva, "Vacuna" table lamps, 16" x 16" . . . . **$600 pair**

Paul Evans, table lamp, 16" x 29.5" **$600**

Brazzoli & Lampa, "Albanella" table lamp, 18" x 21.5" x 18" **$650**

Table lamps, aluminum and chrome, 1960s 17" x 34" **$700 pair**

Gio Ponti, "Bilia" table lamps, 7.5" x 17.25" . . . . **$650 pair**

Castiglioni, large table lamps, Gatto, 13" x 23" . . . . . . **$700 pair**

Murano, glass table lamp, dark purple, white glass, 16" x 14" **$850**

Pierre Cardin, lumico brushed steel table lamp with white glass shade, signed, 10.75" x 10.25" x 4" **$850**

Isamu Noguchi/Knoll, Maple table lamp with cylindrical paper shade, 38.75" x 15.5" x 13". **$900**

Jacques Adnet, figural wooden lamp on enameled metal base, 54" x 13" . . . **$1,000**

Gianfranco Frattini, table lamp, by Luci, 7.5" x 16.5" **$1,000**

James Mont, table lamps, painted wood forms, 8" x 6.5" x 30" . . . . **$800 pair**

Lisa Johansson-Pape, table lamps, large 10" x 17", small 8.75" x 12" . . . . . **$1,000 both**

Gae Aulenti, "Giova" table lamp, 17.5" d x 22" h **$1,400**

James Mont, carved faux tortoise table lamps with spiraled bases and original paper drum shades, 48" x 17" . . . . **$2,500 pair**

Jean Marais, ceramic lamps with sculptural face designs covered in pewter glaze, signed, 17.5" x 5.5" . . . . **$1,800 pair**

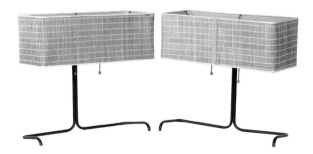

Gerald Thurston, table lamps, 17.5" w x 7" d x 17" h . . . **$3,000 pair**

Arredoluce, bedside table lamps in brass with pierced starbursts to the enameled metal tops, each 13.5" h . . . . **$1,700 pair**

$3,000 to $5,000

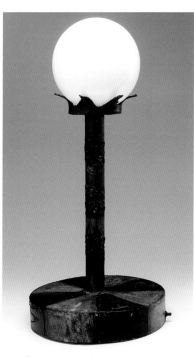

Curtis Jere, crane lamp with adjustable counterweighted arm, of exceptionally large scale, signed C. Jere 1977, 75", arm length approx. 90" **$3,750**

Arredoluce, Triennale lamp with red, yellow and black enameled shades and handles on brass frame; shaft height 61", width as shown 50" **$4,750**

Paul Evans, welded steel ball table lamp with spherical glass shade, circa 1960, 25.5" x 12" **$4,750**

Fontana Arte, brass double-stemmed table lamp on amoeba-shaped plate glass base, with cylindrical linen shades, 29" x 18" x 12" **$4,750**

$5,000 to $10,000

George Nakashima, burlwood lamp with cylindrical parchment shade over a single socket, circa 1969, 29.75" x 16". . . .**$8,000**

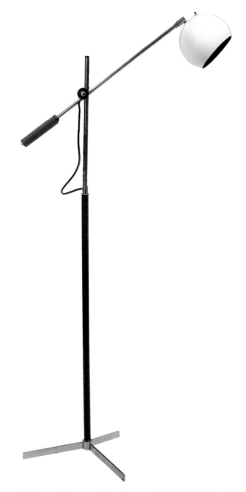

Koch & Lowy torchieres, 19.75" x 66" . . . . **$300 pair**

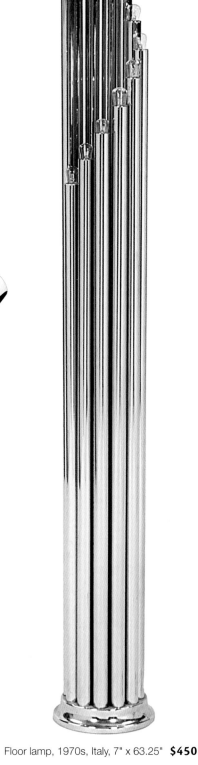

Isamu Noguchi, floor lamp with spherical mulberry paper shade on bamboo shaft with weighted black metal base, 76.5" x 19.5" **$325**

Koch and Lowy, floor lamp, 34" x 63.5", shade 7" **$400**

Floor lamp, 1970s, Italy, 7" x 63.25" **$450**

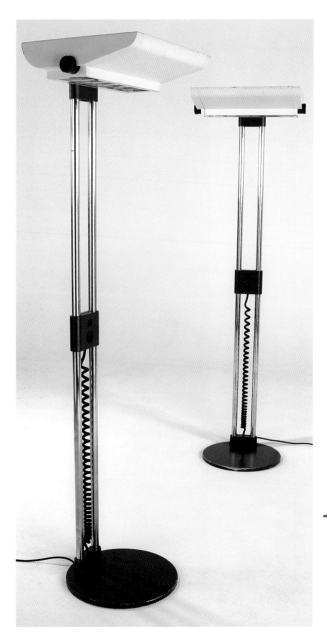

Roland Smith, Victor floor lamp, circa 1948, 48.5" x 44" **$750**

Angelo Cortesi and Sergio Chiappa Catto, Cicindela aluminum floor lamps, 68" x 14" . . . . **$1,000 pair**

Floor lamps, 25.5" x 56". . . . . **$475 pair**

Cedric Hartman, floor lamp, chromed form, 11" x 13" x 37" **$800**

Stilus Milano, aluminum floor lamp with four pivoting sections, and five sockets, approx. 57" x 17" x 12" **$1,000**

Vistosi, floor lamp with eight sockets and blown-glass disc shades, 56.5" x 10.75" **$450**

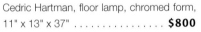

Angelo Cortesi and Sergio Chiappa Catto, Cicindela aluminum floor lamp, 68" x 14" **$1,000**

Casella floor lamp, chromed steel form, 12" w, height adjusts from 32" to 50" **$650**

Koch and Lowy, floor lamp, 34" x 58", shade 7" **$475**

$1,000 to $3,000

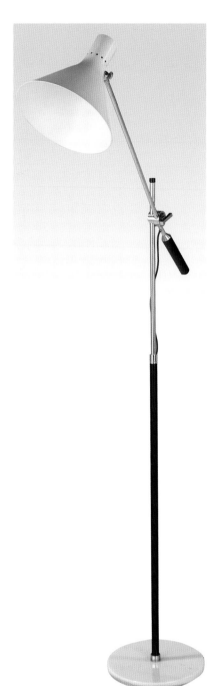

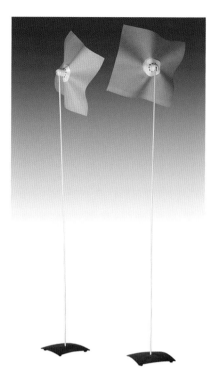

Sergio Brazzoli & Ermanno Lampa, Alba floor lamp, 18" x 23" x 64"...... **$1,700**

Mario Bellini and Giorgio Origlia/Artimede, steel floor lamps with paper shades, 80" x 18" sq............ **$1,400 pair**

Arteluce, adjustable single-arm floor lamp with on marble base, base stamped Made in Italy, 57.5" x 35"............. **$1,100**

Great Grossman/Ralph O. Smith, olive green grasshopper enameled metal floor lamp on tripod base, 50.5" x 15".. **$3,000**

Kazuhide Takahama, Totem floor lamp, 10.25" x 7.5" x 71.5"..........**$1,300**

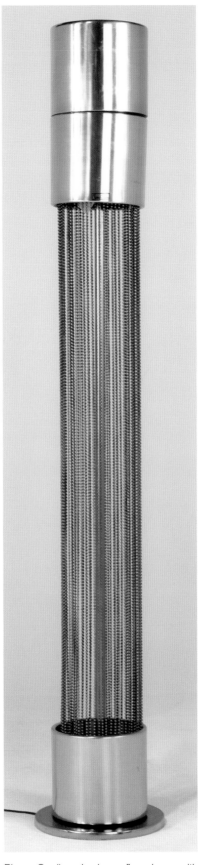

Angelo Lelli, floor lamp, three directional light sources, 12.5" x 79".......**$1,900**

Pierre Cardin, aluminum floor lamp with beaded metal shade, signed Pierre Cardin, 64" x 11" **$2,100**

Robert Mallet-Stevens, steel torchere lamp, commissioned for the Villa Cavrois, Paris, 68.75" x 12" **$2,000**

$3,000 to $5,000

Vladimir Kagan, walnut and brushed chrome floor lamp with string shade and integrated table, branded "A Vladimir Kagan Design", 62.5" x 20", table depth 19.5" **$3,500**

Tommi Parzinger, floor lamps, 6" x 67" . . . . **$4,000 pair**

Marc Newson/Idee, Super Guppy floor lamp in aluminum on casters, IDEE label, 73" x 34" x 30" **$3,500**

Robert Worth, carved and laminated oak floor lamp, branded mark, 1970, 58" x 24" x 21" **$4,500**

Gino Sarfatti/Arteluce, floor lamp, spiraling brass stem with nine adjustable enameled metal shades, stamped Arteluce Made in Italy, 81" x 14"..............**$8,500**

Arredoluce, Triennale floor lamp in brass and enameled metal with three adjustable arms, 59" x 32"...................**$8,000**

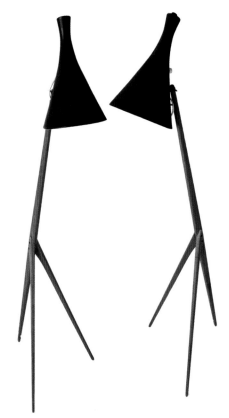

Tommi Parzinger, four-arm painted iron floor lamps with green linen drum shades, 60" x 16".....................**$8,500 pair**

Luxus, teak tripod floor lamps with black enameled shades, Luxus Vittsgo decal, Sweden, 58" x 16.5"..............**$9,000 pair**

Polished brass floor lamp, its adjustable head with frosted glass diffuser, Italy, 80" x 25" x 19" **$9,500**

George Nakashima, Kent Hall rosewood and holly floor lamp with cylindrical paper shade and cruciform base of English and Persian walnut, 57.5" x 16.5". . . .**$10,000**

George Nakashima, walnut floor lamp with white paper shade, 68" x 14.5" **$25,000**

Karl Springer, eight-arm chandeliers of silvered Venetian glass, with polished chrome hardware and ceiling cap, 39" x 39" . . . .**$5,000 pair**

$5,000 to $10,000

Brass and enameled metal elliptical chandelier with floriform motif, Italy, 48.5" x 61.5" **$6,500**

$10,000 and up

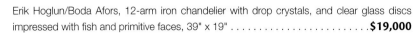

Erik Hoglun/Boda Afors, 12-arm iron chandelier with drop crystals, and clear glass discs impressed with fish and primitive faces, 39" x 19" **$19,000**

Wall Sconces/Lights

$1,000 and under

Lightolier wall sconce, 6" x 11.75" . . . **$200**

Stilnovo, sconces, 7.75" x 10" x 18.5" . . . .**$1,000 pair**

Achille Castigioni/Flos, Toio uplighter with chrome-plated stem and enameled metal base, Atelier International label, 64" **$750**

Nelson, wall lamps, raffia-covered hanging shades, 7.75" x 9.75" ; 23" from shade to wall . . . . **$550 pair**

$1,000 to $3,000

Poul Henningsen, PH outdoor sconce, 12" x 20.5"; shade is 18" **$1,700**

$3,000 to $5,000

Charlotte Perriand, CP1 wall-mount sconces with adjustable enameled metal shades, white, set of eight, 6.5" x 5" x 3" .... **$3,500 set**

Serge Mouille, Cachan enameled metal wall sconce, 11" x 11" x 9.5" **$4,500**

Jean Marais, sculptural bronze sconces with marble shades, signed, 21.5" x 4" .... **$4,000 pair**

Max Ingrand/Fontana Arte, glass wall lights with partially etched Murano glass panels on nickel-plated mounts, 8" x 4.75" x 6" **$9,000 pair**

seating

Armchairs

$1,000 and under

Of all the expressions in Modernist design that you can buy, seating provides the greatest variety of form and function. From the highly artistic and abstract to the most basic and functional, designers and manufacturers embraced the production of chairs and assorted seating like no other piece of furniture. From the beginnings of Modernism to the current day, the big names still carry a certain cachet; Eames, Knoll, Nakashima, Kagan, Noguchi, Saarinen, Perriand. You name the designer and you will see their name somewhere on a chair. The good news is that you can spend as little as $100 and get a great example, or as much as a few hundred thousand dollars for an icon of design. Study hard, learn well and buy the best you can afford and you will never go home disappointed.

Armchairs, brass, faux bamboo frames, light green fabric, 22.5" x 24" x 42" . . . . **$475 pair**

Edward Wormley, armchairs by Dunbar, four, 21.75" x 20.5" x 32", seat 18.5" . . . . **$350 set**

George Nelson, Steelframe chair, 29" x 27" x 27" **$375**

George Nakashima, walnut armchair, 28.5" x 24" x 20" **$800**

Shiro Kuramata, armchair upholstered in gray wool, arms trimmed in grooved rubber, on black enameled steel frame, 29.5" x 20.75" x 20.5"..........**$1,000**

Le Corbusier, LC/1 Basculant chairs brown leather, 25" x 27.5" x 26" .... **$550 pair**

Le Corbusier (1887-1965)

Born Charles-Édouard Jeanneret-Gris, in Switzerland, Le Corbusier is one of the three undisputed founders of Modernism. His influence is hotly debated today and he continues to be a controversial figure in the Modern movement, as much for the fascist leanings of his politics later in life as for his philosophies of urban planning and architecture. What is clear about Le Corbusier, though, is that he played a crucial role in the development of key ideas that influenced Modern designers in the first half of the 20th century. His versatility as a writer, artist, theorist and philosopher were, and still are, evident to this day in the mind-boggling array of buildings, artwork and texts that bear his name.

Le Corbusier's involvement with Modern furniture began in 1928, when he brought Charlotte Perriand into his Paris studio to design the furniture for his architectural projects. Along with his cousin, Pierre Jeanneret, the trio produced the first chrome-plated tubular steel chairs, designed for two of his projects, which arguably introduced Machine-Age philosophy to furniture design. The influence and importance of these creations cannot be overstated. They are still in production, manufactured exclusively by Cassina S.p.A., though they are widely available in copies for much less than an original would cost, especially if that original dates back to the first mass production of the chairs in the early 1930s.

$1,000 to $3,000

Milo Baughman/Thayer Coggin, polished steel armchairs upholstered with woven ecru fabric, 28" x 26.25" x 31.5" . . . .**$1,400 pair**

George Nakashima, walnut armchairs, 28.5" x 25" x 17.5" **$1,500 pair**

Paolo Buffa, mahogany armchairs upholstered in rust-colored velvet, 35" x 22.5" x 17.5". . . . .**$1,500 pair**

Gaetano, Pesce Feltri armchair, by Cassina, 56" x 22" x 39"**$2,000**

Le Corbusier, LC/2 chairs, pair, cream-colored leather, 29.5" x 27.5" x 27" . . . . **$1,900 pair**

Hans Wegner, CH25 armchairs, 28" x 28" x 28" . . . . **$2,000 pair**

Tyco, living room set, pair of single-arm chairs with pedestal side table, floor lamp, ottoman and tray, chairs 32" x 23.75" x 26", table 24" x 24.5" x 14.25", ottoman with tray 20" x 21.5" sq . . . . . **$2,000 set**

Osvaldo Borsani/Tecno, steel reclining chair with rubber armrests, brass hardware marked T, 38" x 28" x 42" **$2,100**

Fruitwood high-back armchairs upholstered in beige and olive textured fabric, Sweden, 50" x 26" x 21" . . . . **$2,200 pair**

Teak wing-back chairs upholstered in cream chenille. Danish control tags, 39" x 34" x 30" . . . . **$2,300 pair**

Franco Albini, early armchairs, six, 21.75" x 23" x 30.5" . . . . **$2,500 set**

George Nakashima, walnut "New Chair" with arms, 39" x 24.5" x 20" **$2,500**

Borge Mogensen, "Spanish" chair, tan leather, dimensions n/a **$2,600**

Shiro Kuramato/XO, "Sing, Sing, Sing" anodized steel armchairs, marked XO, 33.5" x 20.5" x 23.5". . . . . **$2,700 pair**

Finn Juhl , No. 53 easy chair on sculpted rosewood frame upholstered in black vinyl, 29.5" x 28" x 30" **$2,900**

Vladimir Kagan, armchair upholstered in slate gray bias wool, on polished aluminum tripod base, 40" x 27" x 30". **$3,000**

Warren McArthur, aluminum armchairs with cushions covered in wool frise fabric, 33" x 20" x 25". . . . . **$3,000 pair**

$3,000 to $5,000

T.H. Robsjohn-Gibbings armchairs, 27" x 28" x 33" **$5,000 pair**

Armchairs with brass-leather cushions on oak frames with brass-capped feet, 37.5" x 25.25" x 24.25".............**$4,000 pair**

$5,000 to $10,000

Paolo Pallucco, Barba D'Argento armchair with adjustable seat, 28.5" x 20" x 28".................................**$5,000**

Hans Wegner, Papa Bear armchair and ottoman; chair 39" x 35.5" x 34", ottoman 16.5" x 27.5" x 16.5".............**$5,500 both**

Armchairs upholstered in black fabric on parchment-covered framed with brass-capped feet, 31" x 28.5" x 25".........**$6,000 pair**

Hans Wegner/Johannes Hansen/Knoll, oak armchairs with violet and burnt umber cushions, one with Knoll International label, set of four, 32.5" x 27.5" x 22"...................**$5,500 set**

Mario Bellini, "Amanta" modular chairs, brown, five, each 31" x 34" x 25.5" . . . . **$500 set**

Design Research, extended bench with walnut top on steel frame, marked, 15.5" x 84" x 17" **$600**

Mario Bellini, "Amanta" modular chairs, brown/oatmeal, each 33" x 34" x 28" . . . . **$600 pair**

Edward Wormley/Dunbar, ebonized wood bench with brass stretcher, 15.5" x 56" x 18" **$600**

Edward Wormley/Dunbar, ebonized wood bench with brass stretcher, 15.5" x 56" x 18" **$600**

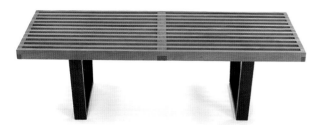

Nelson, Platform Bench, birch top, 48.25" x 18.25" x 14" . . . **$750**

Baker loveseat, armless form, 57" x 34.5" x 30". **$850**

Edward Wormley, vanity seat by Dunbar, 28" x 20" x 22.5". . . **$850**

Peter Stamberg and Paul Aferiat, Salsa settee, 75" x 30" x 29" **$850**

Milo Baughman/Thayer Coggin, long rosewood bench on ebonized
base, Thayer Coggin label, 9.5" x 106" x 24.75" **$1,000**

Don Chadwick, modular seating, moss green fabric, seven pieces, 138" x 64"; each piece at back 27" x 30". . . . . **$1,000 set**

Milo Baughman, bench, walnut frame with hickory dowels, 81" x 18" x 11.5" **$1,200**

Jay Spectre, curved bench with lobed buff leather cushion on laminated oak frame, 29.5" x 64" x 18.5". **$1,250**

Vladimir Kagan, omnibus settee upholstered in striped Knoll fabric on Plexiglas base, re-upholstered in Knoll fabric, 28" x 85" x 32" . . **$1,500**

Vladimir Kagan, omnibus settee upholstered in striped Knoll fabric on Plexiglas base, re-upholstered in Knoll fabric, 28" x 85" x 32" **$1,500**

George Nelson, platform bench by Herman Miller, 102.5" x 18.5" x 14"..........**$1,800**

Borge Mogensen, settee by Fritz Hansen, 33.5" x 29" x 33.75"**$1,800**

Settee, upholstered in light blue silk on sculpted, winged frame, Italy, 36" x 66" x 32"..................................**$2,000**

Tommi Parzinger, settee upholstered in green leather on ebonized wood base, 33.5" x 55" x 29"..........................**$3,000**

Eero Saarinen/Knoll, womb settee upholstered in green fabric on black metal frame, 35" x 60" x 32"................... **$3,250**

Charlotte Perriand, pine bench seats, five, 16.5" x 63" x 11.75", 16.5" x 49" x 11.75" and 16.5" x 17.5" x 11.75" ..... **$3,250 set**

James Mont, settee with ebonized fretwork frame, upholstered in patterned fabric, 26" x 54" x 34" **$4,500**

Maison Jansen, antiqued silver settee with tufted back upholstered in black silk, signed, 35.5" x 46" x 24"................ **$4,000**

Marco Zanusi, "Lady" settee upholstered in caramel suede with cream leather trim, on flaring brass legs, 39" x 61" x 31"........ **$5,000**

$5,000 to $10,000

"Safari" seating unit from Archizoom Associati, three pieces; 101.5" x 101.5" x 25", each 50.75" x 50.75" x 25" . . . **$5,500 set**

Finn Juhl/Niels Vodder, sculpted teak settee upholstered in tan leather, branded mark, 23.5" x 55" x 25" **$6,500**

$10,000 and up

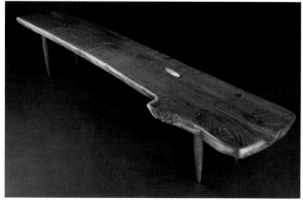

Phillip Lloyd Powell, walnut long bench with legs mortised through the top, 15" x 94" x 18" **$15,000**

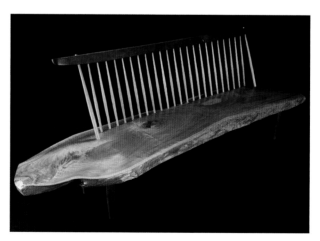

George Nakashima, Conoid bench with back in butternut, free-edge seat with single rosewood butterfly key, 31.5" x 90" x 23" **$32,500**

While some of the most famous examples of Modern design are couches and sofas, the overall output of these has yet to have a strong following. While affordable to most level of buyer, be prepared to pay upwards of $30,000 and $40,000 for the best pieces. There are, however, good sofas and couches available under $1,000 dollars that feature some of the best names in the business, including Ello, Hvidt and Florence Knoll.

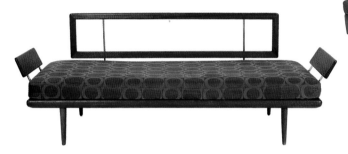

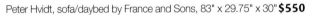

Peter Hvidt, sofa/daybed by France and Sons, 83" x 29.75" x 30" **$550**

Bertha Schaefer, sofa, green wool, 88" x 35" x 31" **$100**

Ello, even-arm sofa upholstered in ivory velvet, with mirrored front panels, 25" x 86" x 36" **$600**

Jens Risom, sofa by Jens Risom Design Inc., 62" x 33.75" x 30"**$750**

Florence Knoll, sofa by Knoll, 84" x 28" x 31" **$800**

Florence Knoll, sofa by Knoll, 84" x 28" x 31" **$800**

Peter Hvidt and Orla Mølgaard-Nielsen, sofa, 112" x 36" x 31", marble is 31.72" x 33" **$800**

Kazuhide Takahama, "Suzanne" sofa, green wool, 95.5" x 33" x 26.75" **$1,000**

Vladimir Kagan, omnibus sofa upholstered in striped Knoll fabric on Plexiglas base, reupholstered in Knoll fabric, 27.5" x 72" x 32" **$1,000**

Vladimir Kagan (1927-)

Few Modern designers can lay claim to as storied a career as Kagan. The German-born American has been a presence on the scene since the early 1950s and has worked with a consistency that would be the envy of any designer of any form. Lucky for aficionados of Modernism, Kagan has remained true to 20th-century design, and, now into his 80s, shows no sign of slowing his pace of work. Kagan is one of those modern designers that are not known so much for a specific piece of furniture as much as his entire philosophy of design. He has been referred to by the New York Times as the "creative grandfather of a whole new generation of designers."

The sharp curves and arching lines of Kagan's furniture are easy to recognize, and no designer or collector worth their salt could miss a piece of his furniture. The result is that prices for his work, especially his early designs, bring several thousand dollars every time they come on the block at auction. Most highly prized are his dining and side-chair sets, as well as his cabinetry and credenzas. Kagan first was brought to international attention when he designed the Delegate's Cocktail Lounge at the United Nations. His most enduring work was his furniture designed for Monsanto's "House of the Future" at Disneyland. Kagan continues to design new lines of furniture to this day, operating out of his Midtown Manhattan studio, and released his newest line of couture in spring of 2008.

$1,000 to $3,000

Florence Knoll, early sofa by Knoll, 91" x 30" x 29" **$1,200**

Le Corbusier, LC 3 sofa, 67" x 32" x 23" **$1,200**

Arne Vodder/Bovirke, teak sofa upholstered in olive wool, branded mark, 33.25" x 71" x 24" **$1,500**

Jens Risom Design Inc. sofa, 80" x 30" x 32.5" **$1,400**

Vladimir Kagan/Directional, curvilinear sofa upholstered in grey ultra-suede, Directional label, 29" x 88" x 55" **$2,000**

Vladimir Kagan/Directional, curvilinear sofa upholstered in grey ultras-uede, Directional label, 29" x 94" x 40.5" **$2,000**

Harvey Probber, sofa, tan ultra-suede, 96" x 34" x 25" . . . **$2,000**

Edward Wormley, sofa by Dunbar, 90" x 32" x 28.5" **$2,300**

Knoll, three-seat sofas on tapering birch legs, each 30" x 90" x 29" . . . . **$2,600 pair**

Edward Wormley/Dunbar, sofa upholstered in Jack Lenor Larsen fabric, on walnut base, 27.5" x 100" x 31" **$3,000**

Marco Zanusi/Pizzetti, adjustable sofa/chaise lounge upholstered in finely ribbed red fabric on brass legs, size closed 31.5" x 73" x 33" **$3,000**

Gio Ponti, sofa on ebonized wood feet, upholstered in yellow wool, 31" x 71" x 25" **$3,000**

Paul Evans, burlwood patchwork sofa upholstered in brown suede, an original Paul Evans brass tag, 26.5" x 78" x 32" **$3,750**

Vladimir Kagan, 100B loveseat upholstered in woven khaki fabric on black enameled wood legs, 36" x 60" x 33". **$3,250**

Parzinger, "American Modern" sectional sofa, leopard print fabric, 109" x 30.5" x 28". **$5,000**

Charles Eames/Herman Miller, group lounge sofa with channeled black leather upholstery, 33.5" x 73" x 30". **$5,000**

$5,000 to $10,000

Curved sofa upholstered in champagne chenille on oak feet, French, 34" x 92" x 47" **$6,500**

Wharton Esherick, sectional sofa upholstered in cream textured fabric, two-piece, 39" x 81" x 39" and 39" x 76" x 39" **$7,500**

$10,000 and up

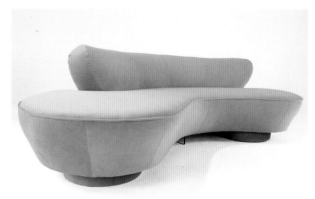

Vladimir Kagan /Directional, cloud sofa upholstered in golden velvet on two covered circular bases and single Lucite fin, Directional label, 39" x 81" x 39" and 39" x 76" x 39" **$11,000**

Vladimir Kagan, curved 6999 sofa upholstered in cream chenille on Plexiglas base, 29.5" x 108" x 32" **$12,000**

Alexander Girard/Herman Miller, sofa covered in mocha, tan and white leather with brown and white-checkered cushions, 26.5" x 84.75" x 28" **$14,000**

Vladimir Kagan/Dreyfuss, curved floating sofa upholstered in indigo wool, on sculpted walnut frame, 27.5" x 90" x 28.5" **$18,000**

Vladimir Kagan, wide-angle sofa upholstered in chocolate chenille on sculpted walnut legs, 30" x 112" x 32" **$17,000**

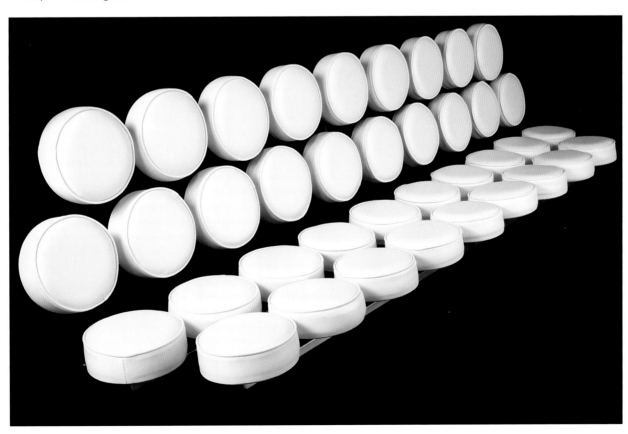

Irving Harper/George Nelson and Associates, Marshmallow sofa upholstered in white vinyl on brushed and enameled steel frame, signed Irving Harper (possibly the most famous Modernist sofa ever made), 30.5" x 103" x 30" **$37,500**

Desk/Dining Chairs

$1,000 and under

Brown Saltman, dining chairs, four, string backs, 18.25" w x 22" d x 32" h...... **$275 set**

Jorgen Rasmussen, desk chair, blue wool,
23" x 23" x 32" **$250**

Harry Bertoia, chairs, set of four, 21" x 20"x 30.5" .... **$325 set**

Thonet, chairs, four, 19" x 20" x 30" .... **$325 set**

Glostrup Mobelfabrik, dining chairs, Denmark, four, 24.75" x 21" x 30.5".. **$400 set**

Mart Stam, dining chairs, four, 19" w x 24" d x 31.25" h. . . . . **$400 set**

Charles and Ray Eames, dining or desk-height, wire-seat, rod-base chairs, two, 19"x 18.5" x 32" . . . . **$450 pair**

Greta Grossman, dining chairs, 18" x 20" x 29.5" . . . . **$550 set**

Dining chairs, four, black leather upholstery, 1960s, 19"x 18" x 32" . . . . **$475 set**

Dining chairs, maker unknown covered in brown suede on brass and chromed steel bases, set of six, 43" x 16.5" x 18.5"..... **$750 set**

Dining chairs with buff-colored vinyl cushions on parchment-covered frames, set of six, 41.5" x 18.5" x 18" .... **$1,000 set**

Harvey Probber, dining chairs, side 21.25" x 24" x 32", arm 21.75"................................. **$1,000 all**

Ron Seff, dining chairs, eight, 23" x 20" x 33".......... **$750 set**

Charles and Ray Eames, metal dining chairs, four, 19.5" x 21" x 29.5"................................... **$1,000 set**

Jean Prouve, oak plywood office chair on adjustable steel base, 34.5" x 15.75" x 18" **$1,000**

Piretti, "Plona" folding chair, 27" x 21" x 29"............**$50**   Jack Heany, Aluma-Stack chairs, six, 18" x 22" x 32"... **$250 set**

Overman, AB Tango chairs, four, 17.75" x 17" x 28.75".. **$100 set**

Ray Komai chair, 21" x 18.75" x 29.5" **$350**   Harry Bertoia, Diamond chairs, orange vinyl and orange fabric, two, larger 43" x 30" x 27.5", smaller 34" x 28" x 29.75"... **$475 pair**

Mario Botta, "Latonda 614" chairs, 25" x 18.5" x 29.5"... **$600 pair**

Charles and Ray Eames, shell chair, 25" x 24.5" x 27.5" **$600**

Eero Saarinen/Knoll, womb chair upholstered in blue fabric, on chrome base, 36" x 38.5" x 34"......................**$700**

Vladimir Kagan, omnibus chair upholstered in striped Knoll fabric, complete with bolster, on Plexiglas base, reupholstered in Knoll fabric, 27.5" x 31" x 32"...........................**$800**

Vernor Panton, cone chair, purple wool seat pad, 25" x 22" x 29" **$900**

Eero Saarinen/Knoll, early womb chair and ottoman upholstered in original off-white canvas, Knoll Associates label, 27.5" x 31" x 32" **$1,100**

Jorgen Hovelskov, Harp chair with mahogany frame and flag line seat, 54" x 44" x 40" **$1,250**

George Nelson/Herman Miller, coconut chair upholstered in black boucle, 34" x 40" x 29" **$1,500**

Andrew Willner, American School chair, 22.5" x 24" x 41.5" **$1,400**

Osvaldo Borsani, chairs, large sculptural forms, brown, 35" x 37" x 29". . . . . .**$1,500 pair**

Boriek Sipek, sculptural rattan chair, 36" x 35.25" x 24.25" . . . **$1,800**

Pierre Paulin, ribbon chair and round ottoman, black, chair 40" x 30" x 27.5", ottoman 21" x 15.5" **$2,200**

Hans Wegner/Johannes Hansen, peacock chair on ash frame with teak armrests and woven cord seat, branded Johannes Hansen Copenhagen Denmark, 42" x 30" x 25" **$1,900**

Eero Saarinen/Knoll, womb chair and ottoman upholstered in dark grey leather, with Knoll label, chair 36" x 38.5" x 34" **$2,200**

Frank O. Gehry/Easy Edges, corrugated cardboard Wiggle Chairs, 33.5" x 15.5" x 22" . . . . **$2,500 pair**

Eero Saarinen/Knoll, two womb chairs and ottomans upholstered in burnt orange and brown fabric, on black metal frames; chairs 36" x 38.5" x 34" . . . . . **$2,900 all**

Arne Jacobsen, Seagull chairs in original white finish, marked in Denmark by Fritz Hansen 1972, 31.5" x 21.5" x 18" . . . . **$3,000 pair**

Aarne Jacobsen (1902-1971)

Truly the Crown Prince of Danish Modernism, Jacobsen was a prolific architect and a revolutionary designer who left an architectural imprint on most every continent. Except for a few years of World War II that he spent in Sweden, Jacobsen was fiercely loyal to Denmark. His architecture was a fusion of perfect balance, obsessive detail and complete harmony. To lovers of Modern furniture design, however, mention the name of Arne Jacobsen and four chairs come straight to mind: The Ant, The Egg, The Swan and Model 3107 – Series 7. If you know already, then that's enough. If you don't, then you soon will. With these four massively important chair designs, Jacobsen sold more than 5 million pieces in his lifetime, and many more in the ensuing decades since his death.

Jacobsen was already a renowned figure in Denmark when he burst onto the Modern scene in the mid-1950s. His furniture designs are still widely copied and respected, and original examples of any of his four iconic pieces are most likely going to be hard to find, quite expensive, and worth every penny. It is the Model 3107 – Series 7 Chair that set off the true design revolution when, in 1963, photographer Richard Morley grabbed a knockoff of the 3107 that was in his studio, sat a half-naked Christine Keeler in it and took what would emerge as one of the most important, iconic and copied photographs of the 20th century. It set off a frenzy among the buying public to get one of the Model 3107 – Series 7 chairs. Stanley Kubrick did much the same for Jacobsen's stainless steel flatware, originally designed for the SAS Ari Terminal and Royal Hotel in Copenhagen, when he chose them as his futuristic utensils in 2001: A Space Odyssey.

$3,000 to $5,000

Paul Evans, 202 corrugated cardboard dining chairs with burlap covering, complete with original box and instructions, circa 1978, assembled size 34" x 18" x 27" . . . . **$3,250 pair**

Arne Jacobsen, Seagull chair covered in brown leather on steel frame, marked in Denmark by Fritz Hansen 1972, 31.5" x 21.5" x 18" **$4,750**

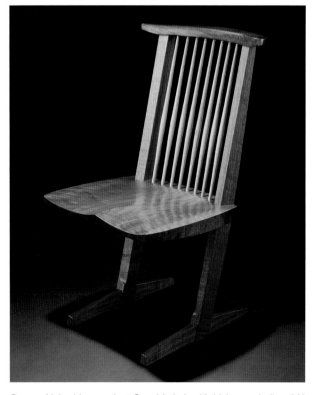

$5,000 to $10,000

George Nakashima, walnut Conoid chair with hickory spindles, 36" x 20.5" x 21.5" **$5,000**

Phillip Lloyd Powell, New Hope chair in walnut with webbed seat support, 32" x 29.5" x 30.5" **$7,500**

George Nakashima, walnut Conoid cushion chair with hickory spindles, 34" x 35" x 31.5" **$11,000**

Paul Evans, sculpted bronze chair with orange crushed velvet upholstery, 31.75" x 28.75" x 24.75" **$11,000**

Hans Wegner/Johannes Hansen, peacock chairs in ash and teak with woven cord seats, branded marks, set of six, 42.25" x 27.25" x 21.25" . . . . **$12,000 set**

George Nakashima, walnut Conoid dining chairs with hickory spindles, set of four, 35.25" x 20" x 21" . . . . **$25,000 set**

Wendell Castle, sculpted oak sleigh chair with hard leather sling seat, 1963, signed WC 63, 34.5" x 29" x 51.5" **$170,000**

Lounge Chairs
$1,000 and under

Charles and Ray Eames, La Fonda chairs, blue wool, 18.5" x 16" x 31.75" .... **$300 pair**

Pierre Paulin, 303 lounge chair, red seat pad, 32" x 30" x 24" **$100**

Paul Laszlo, lounge chairs, tan velour, 24" x 27" x 27.5" **$300 pair**

Lounge chair, dark gray leather seat and olive green chenille backrest, 1980s, 30" w x 46" d x 31" h. **$300**

George Nakashima, walnut "New" chair, 36" x 18.5" x 17" **$1,600**

Edward Wormley/Dunbar, lounge chair and ottoman upholstered in tan suede on brushed brass legs, chair 31" x 25" x 32" **$1,600**

Edward Wormley/Dunbar, pair of lounge chairs upholstered in original marigold chenille, fabric tags, 33" x 30.25" x 30.25" . . . . **$1,700 pair**

Eero Saarinen/Knoll, grasshopper chair with corduroy upholstery, 34.5" x 27" x 32.5" **$1,800**

Selig, lounge chairs, 40" x 37" seat 13" . . . . **$1,800 pair**

Geoffrey Harcourt, lounge chairs, 28" x 28" x 27" . . . .**$1,900 pair**

John Hutton/Randolph & Hein, lounge chair in white painted finish with carved paw feet, 31.5" x 25" x 27". **$1,900**

Eero Saarinen/Knoll, grasshopper chair with fabric upholstery, 25.5" x 26.25" x 29". **$1,900**

Erwin and Estelle Laverne, Daffodil Lucite lounge chairs from the Invisible Group series, with yellow seat pads, 29.5" x 35.25" x 26.25". . . . .**$2,000 pair**

Harvey Probber, caned mahogany barrel-back lounge chairs, 24" x 31" x 28". . . . . **$2,000 pair**

Charles and Ray Eames, wooden lounge chair, red aniline-dyed molded birch plywood, 22" x 24" x 26.75". **$2,000**

Peter Karpf, "Wing" lounge chair, 49" x 32" x 25.5" **$2,500**

Alvar Aalto, early C chair, 30" x 32" x 28.5" **$2,500**

Rene Gabriel, oak lounge chairs, pickled, with slatted seats, 30" x 21" x 40" . . . . **$2,900 pair**

Knoll, cube lounge chairs upholstered in Knoll checkered fabric on steel bases, 30" x 32.5" x 31.5" . . . . **$2,900 pair**

$3,000 to $5,000

Hans Wegner/Getama, adjustable oak lounge chair/daybed and matching ottoman, both with original spring covers and gray wool cushions, branded marks, 34" x 48" x 29". **$3,250**

Warren Platner/Knoll, lounge chair and ottoman upholstered in original mottled blue and black fabric on black wire frames, 39" x 41" x 36" **$3,500**

Charles and Ray Eames/Herman Miller, rosewood lounge chair and ottoman with black leather upholstery, 32" x 33" x 30" **$3,500**

Poul Kjaerholm/E. Kold Christensen, PK22 lounge chairs covered in tan leather on steel bases, impressed marks, set of four, 28" x 25" x 25" . . . . **$4,250 set**

Poul Kjaerholm (1929-1980)

As important as any other graduate of the Danish School, Poul Kjaerholm ranks today as one of the most prolific, popular and enduring designers to ever embraced the Machine-Age aesthetic. His "PK" line of chairs, tables, stools, chaise lounges, daybeds and sofas are among the most desirable and— happily—widely available examples of Modern design on the market today. Kjaerholm not only embraced the use of steel in conjunction with other "natural" materials, he saw steel as having a full life and energy of its own. Obviously, consumers agreed and made several of his designs among the most successful, and copied, in history.

One of the standard bearers of Danish Mid-Century Modernism, along with van der Rohe, Wegner and Risom, Kjaerholm meshed his philosophy of good, comfortable design with 20th-century mass-production techniques. The result was that he became a recognized and respected designer across the globe, but also beloved as a national treasure in his native Denmark. He was barely four years into his career running the Danish National Academy of Art, after 20 years of teaching there, when he died at the age of 51 in 1980.

Warren Platner/Knoll, lounge chair and ottoman upholstered in original Alexander Girard ochre fabric, on black wire frames, Knoll Associates tags, chair 39" x 41" x 29" **$4,250**

Herbert Von Thaden, tall-back reclining chair, 19.75" x 34.5" x 38" **$4,750**

F.A. Porsche, reclining lounge chair with black leather upholstery on arched metal frame, stamped IP84S Design F.A. Porsche, with Made in Germany label, 44" x 29" x 44" **$5,000**

Paul Laszlo/Glenn of California, bleached mahogany lounge chairs with woven cane seats and backs, 30" x 28" x 28"....**$5,500 pair**

Poul Kjaerholm/E. Kold Christensen, PK9 chairs upholstered in black leather, on brushed chrome legs, stamped cipher and Denmark, 32" x 20" x 19" ....**$6,500 pair**

Erwin and Estelle Laverne, Daffodil Lucite lounge chairs from the Invisible Group series, with leopard print seat pads, 29.5" x 35.25" 26.25"..........................**$5,500 pair**

Arne Norell, lounge chairs with brown leather seats on teak frames, Norell cloth tags, 29" x 32" x 32"...................**$6,500 pair**

Marco Zanusi, senior lounge chairs upholstered in eggshell leather with brass legs, 41" x 30" x 30"......**$6,500 pair**

Phillip Lloyd Powell, New Hope chair, 32" x 29.5" x 30.5"................**$8,500**

Osvaldo Borsani /Tecno, reclining chaise with olive chenille cushion (not shown), Tecno Made in Italy label, 36" x 36" x 75" **$13,000**

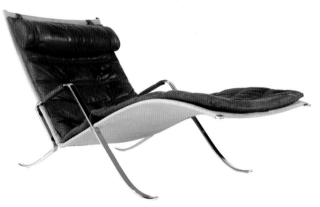

Preben Fabricius and Jorgen Kastholm/Alfred Kill, grasshopper lounge chair on polished steel frame upholstered in channeled brown leather with canvas sling support, 32.5" x 28.25" x 57" **$14,000**

Finn Juhl/Niels Vodder, chieftain chair with reddish-brown leather cushions on teak frame, branded mark, 27" x 40.5" x 29" **$32,500**

Rockers

Herman Miller, rocking chairs, 23" x 27" x 29" . . . . **$700 pair**

Charles and Ray Eames, molded plastic rocker, red-orange, 24.75" x 27" x 27"**$550**

L. Meher, custom walnut plywood and steel rocker, signed L. Meher 78, 37.5" x 21.5" x 30" **$1,000**

Charles and Ray Eames, molded plastic rocker, yellow, 24.25" x 27" x 26.25"**$750**

Hans Wegner, early rocking chair, 24.25" x 30" x 30" **$2,400**

Charles and Ray Eames, molded plastic rocker, gray Zenith, rope-edge, 24.75" x 27" x 27" **$1,900**

Lucite vanity stool, upholstered seat, 1950s, 22" x 12" x 17" **$100**

Jorgen Rasmussen, stool, red wool, 25" x 17" **$250**

Eero Saarinen, pedestal stool, gold wool, 15" x 16" **$350**

Miyoko Ito, garden stool, ceramic with drip glaze, 12" x 16" **$750**

Barstools, post-modern, multi-colored vinyl, 14" x 26". **$950**

Rosengren Hansen, bar stools, 14" x 15" x 35.5", seat height is 28.5" .... **$1,200 pair**

Poul Henningsen, tubular steel piano stool with original red leatherette seat, 20" x 14.25". **$1,600**

Paul McCobb, stools, off-white brushed vinyl, 20" x 20" x 17". .... **$1,900 pair**

Isamu Noguchi/Knoll, teak rocking stool with steel wire frame, circa 1954, 10.5" x 14" **$5,500**

Wharton Esherick, three-legged sculpted walnut stool, signed WE 1968, 20" x 14" x 21.75" **$6,500**

$10,000 and up

Isamu Noguchi/Herman Miller, rare "Rudder" stool, model no. IN-22, birch with two tubular steel legs, unmarked, 17" x 20.5" **$20,000**

shelving, storage

Also see Desks, Credenzas

$1,000 and under

It's remarkable that Modernist design didn't produce a greater array of storage units and bookshelves, given that some of the most iconic symbols of Modern design – Eames storage units, Perriand biblioteques and Evans cabinetry – come in the form. That's not to say that there isn't a wide variety on the market. There is indeed, just nowhere near as many as you see in tables and chairs. Marked by a liberal use of color and open space, bookshelves and storage are a mode that big-name designers were able to cut loose on a little bit, and are still a great place for the neophyte to get started for a few hundred dollars. The advanced collectors may hone their sensibilities from the high five figures into the mid-six-figure range.

Chest, 1940s, by Plymouth, 30" x 19.75" x 33.5" **$250**

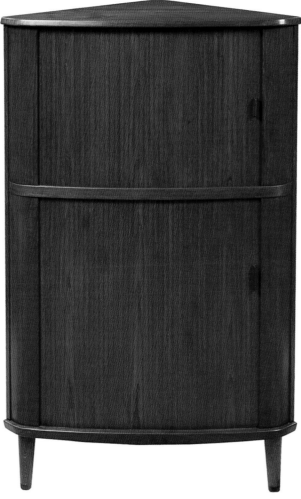

George Nelson, display cabinet, 34" x 12" d x 23" **$200**

Skovmand & Andersen, corner cabinet, 36.5" x 25.5" x 61.25" **$375**

Cabinets, Donald Deskey style, exotic wood veneer, each 36" x 14.75" x 21" .... **$425 pair**

George Nelson, Basic Series cabinets, 34" x 18.5" x 24" **$550 pair**

Hans Wegner (attributed), cabinet, 25.5" x 14" x 27.75" **$425**

Renzo Rutili, cabinet, 100.75" x 20.25" x 31" **$550**

George Nelson, cabinet by Herman Miller, 24" x 18.5" x 29.75" **$600**

George Nelson, bookcase, 34" x 12" x 23.5" **$600**

Edmund Spence, cabinet, one center door, 72" x 20" x 32" **$600**

Seth Ben Ali, mahogany cabinet, circa 1940, 42" x 19.5" x 32" **$650**

Paul McCobb, cabinet by Calvin, 1960s, 36" x 19" x 34.25" **$650**

George Nelson, Steelframe cabinet, 33.5" x 17" x 29.5" **$650**

Walnut stereo cabinet with interior Garrard record player and television compartment, Scandinavian, 32" x 54" x 21" **$750**

George Nelson, Steelframe cabinet, 33.5" x 17" x 29.5" **$800**

Bernini cabinet, Italy, rosewood case with two doors, four drawers, and a drop-front door with one shelf and open storage, birch lined interior and finished back, ebonized wood pulls, 47.25" x 16.5" x 58" **$800**

John Kapel, sideboard, 80" x 20" x 30" **$800**

Harvey Probber, wall cabinet, 30" x 19.75" x 33.5".................**$1,000**

Florence Knoll, Executive Collection cabinet, 37.75" x 18" x 25.25"...........**$900**

Vladimir Kagan, walnut wall-hanging, three-tier shelf with antiqued mirrored back, 35" x 21.25" x 17"............**$1,000**

George Nelson, cabinet by Herman Miller, 40" x 18.5" x 39.75" **$1,100**

Florence Knoll, cabinet, 36" x 17.75" x 27.5" **$1,100**

Eliel Saarinen, cabinet with parquetry drop-front door on either side concealing a mirrored interior with two shelves, over lower shelf on casters, unmarked, 42" x 36" x 18" **$1,100**

Vladimir Kagan, walnut serving cabinet with two doors enclosing two drawers, 31.25" x 48" x 19" **$1,250**

Vladimir Kagan, walnut chest with eight drawers, 36" x 72" x 18" **$1,250**

Edward Wormley/Dunbar, bleached mahogany server with sliding doors enclosing interior pull-out shelves on bentwood legs, Dunbar paper tag, 34" x 42" x 21" **$1,250**

Paul Evans, wall console and mirror; mirror 70.25" h x 20.5" w, console 36.25" x 14.25" x 6" **$1,200**

Florence Knoll, cabinets, dimensions n/a . . . . **$1,400 pair**

Wall unit, rosewood, 1960, 87" x 16.5" x 73" **$1,400**

Robsjohn-Gibbings, cabinet, five drawers, 54" x 20.5" x 32.75".....................................**$1,400**

Herman Miller, Executive Office Group cabinet, 74" x 18.75" x 27"...**$1,400**

Peggy Day/Modern House, chest with six drawers in white enamel with black enameled pulls and pedestal base, branded "A Peggy Day Original For Modern House", 33.25" x 68" x 18.5".........**$1,500**

Pierre Cardin, cabinets in white laminate with chrome trim, each fitted with six interior drawers, signed Pierre Cardin, 51" x 38" x 19"............................**$1,500 pair**

James Mont, oak bar with carved fretwork over red-painted panels and rear shelf, 30" x 92" x 21"........................**$1,500**

Alvar Aalto, early cabinet, birch, five drawers, 31" x 17.5" x 27.75" **$1,600**

Harvey Probber, mahogany veneer faceted side table cabinets, Harvey Probber metal tags, each, 22.25" x 28.5" ... **$1,600 pair**

Edward Wormley, cabinets, each 46" x 20" x 31.25".... **$1,700 pair**

Edward Wormley, sideboard, 59.25" x 18" x 28.25".. **$1,600**

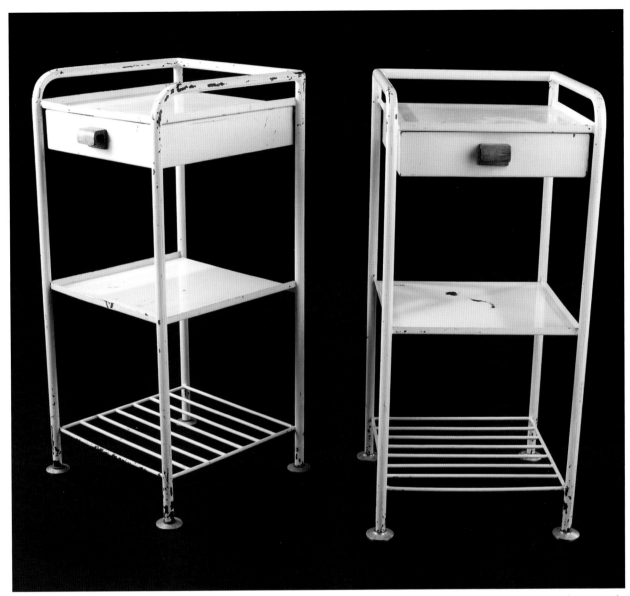

Jean Prouve, white enameled metal single-drawer stands, each 46" x 20" x 31.25" . . . . **$1,800 pair**

Jean Prouve (1901-1984)

Jean Prouve was, until the 1990s, the best early Modern designer that nobody had heard of. He experienced a resurgence when Modernism became hip, and several auction houses began featuring his work. He is now well represented in museums and at auction, and widely recognized as one of the key driving forces behind applying the ideas of the machine age to design without losing aesthetic value. As with so many of the great Modernists, Prouve tended to think of himself as more of an engineer than a designer. This served him extremely well in his collaborations, especially those with Charlotte Perriand, Pierre Jeanneret, Eugene Beaudoin and Marcel Lods.

While influential in many ways to the design and production of furniture today, it was his 1934 introduction of the Standard Chair, a masterpiece of engineering for comfort and sleekness of design, that seems to be where his greatest contribution lies. His collaborations with Perriand and Jeanneret, specifically those for Cité Universitaire in Paris, are equally as influential and equally sought after.

George Nelson, Thin Edge cabinet, 34" x 18.5" x 33.5" **$1,900**

Paul McCobb, wall unit, two pieces, 60.25" x 19.25" x 76.25" **$2,200**

Milo Baughman, chest with two trompe l'oeil doors and four drawers, under a travertine top, 34" x 56" x 19" **$2,000**

Parchment-covered, four-drawer chest with brass pulls and brass-capped feet, 29" x 41" x 31" **$2,300**

George Nelson, Thin Edge cabinet, 56" x 18.5" x 39.75" **$2,600**

Raymond Loewy, DF-2000 cabinet, 41" x 20" x 29.5" **$2,600**

$3,000 to $5,000

George Nakashima/Widdicomb, gentleman's cabinet with walnut case and burlwood door, stamped Nakashima with Widdicomb cloth tag, 9.5" x 47" x 22.25".....**$3,500**

Charles and Ray Eames/Herman Miller, first edition ESU 251, circa 1952, 33.5" x 23.5" x 16"...............**$3,750**

Paul Evans, Aluco Bond cabinet with burled walnut doors, 30" x 39.5" x 18". **$3,750**

Paul Evans (1931-1987)

Known as much for his sculpture and art as for his furniture, Paul Evans was another American designer of the middle part of the 20th century that came out of the Cranbrook Academy of Art in Bloomfield Hills, Mich. Evans is closely associated with the American Craft Movement. Much of his work was designed under the auspices of influential manufacturer Directional Furniture starting in 1964.

It was Evans' feel for metal that set him apart from his Modernist contemporaries. He sculpted his furniture with metal, making a particular splash with his 1950s copper chests and his sculpted steel-front cabinets. Highly sought after today, in large part because he signed most every piece, Evans set a particular standard for the relationship between designer and manufacturer. At Directional Furniture, he insisted every piece be made by hand, finished by hand and supervised by the artist at each step of production. Evans' designs can still be found at auction, shows and shops, especially his furniture lines like the Argente and Sculpted Bronze series, and the ever-popular Cityscape series. His early signed and dated examples can bring anywhere from $10,000 to $75,000 at auction today.

James Mont, cabinet in red lacquer with two doors enclosing five drawers, branded James Mont Design, 32.5" x 48" x 15.5" **$4,000**

Bookcase, pickled oak, with hinged bookstand over three caned shelves, 51.75" x 22.5" x 16" **$4,250**

Charles and Ray Eames/Herman Miller, first edition ESU 201, circa 1952, 32.75" x 47" x 16" **$4,250**

George Nakashima, walnut double chest of drawers with trapezoidal free-edge top, 1959, 32" x 71" x 21"..............**$14,000**

George Nakashima, early walnut chest of drawers in dovetailed case construction, with seven drawers and a pullout shelf, four drawers with bitterroot pulls, 32" x 48" x 20"..............**$14,000**

George Nakashima, walnut Kornblut case with burlwood pull and single interior shelf, 22" x 19" x 19"..............**$14,000**

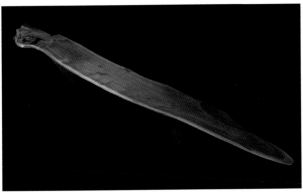

Phillip Lloyd Powell, walnut freeform wall-hanging shelf with ebony butterfly key, 13" x 80" x 10"..............**$14,000**

R & Y Augousti, green shagreen demi-lune cabinet fitted with interior shelves and three-drawer felt-lined jewelry chest, Augousti brass tag, 69.5" x 40" x 17.5"..............**$15,000**

George Nakashima, walnut hanging wall case with grilled sliding doors and overhanging free-edge top, 18.25" x 72" x 18" **$15,000**

Paul Evans /Directional, sculpted bronze disc bar with fitted interior, 72" x 72" x 16" **$18,000**

Wharton Esherick, curved sculpted walnut music cabinet, signed WE '55. Accompanied by "As I Watch'd the Ploughman Ploughing," illustrated by Esherick, inscribed and signed, "For the music shelves of Ruth and Larry. December 1955. Affectionately, Wharton", 23.5" x 41" x 18" **$24,000**

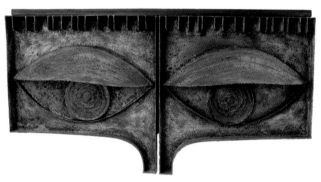

Paul Evans, wall-hanging welded steel eye cabinet, patinated and painted with colored pigments, signed Paul Evans 66, 24" x 48" x 17" **$60,000**

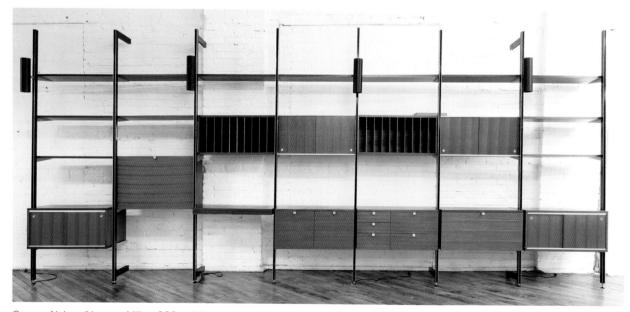

George Nelson/Herman Miller, CSS unit in rosewood veneer and brushed metal, with eight vertical supports, four black enameled metal light fixtures and numerous drawers, cupboards and shelves, 95" x 226" x 18.5" **$20,000**

Charlotte Perriand and Jean Prouve, bibliotheque with enameled aluminum and pine shelving unit on pine long bench, 1953, 63.5" x 138" x 21" **$70,000**

Charlotte Perriand (1903-1999)

Perriand was a woman in a man's world when she joined the atelier of Le Corbusier in Paris in 1927. Yet to reduce the greatness of her work, and the genius of her designs, by looking at them only in the context of the men she worked with is a great disservice. With Le Corbusier, and Pierre Jeanneret, they created the first tubular metal chaise and lounge chairs for the 1929 Salon d'Automne. It could be argued that these were the first truly great, truly Modern pieces of furniture, a trio of design whose effect is still being felt, and seen, to this day.

For Perriand, it was simply the beginning. She quickly became a respected figure in her own right, traveled the world, and incorporated elements of design from every country she visited and worked in, especially Japan – where she worked before World War II – and Vietnam, where she waited out the war after being denied a visa back to France. For three decades, Perriand designed furniture all over the world, of all kinds, and today her work is still in production. Original examples bearing her name, especially the wonderful "biblioteques" that came out several Swiss ski chalets, can command upwards of $200,000 at auction. That makes Perriand one of the first among equals in the pantheon of Modern Design. An important lady, certainly, but a more important designer.

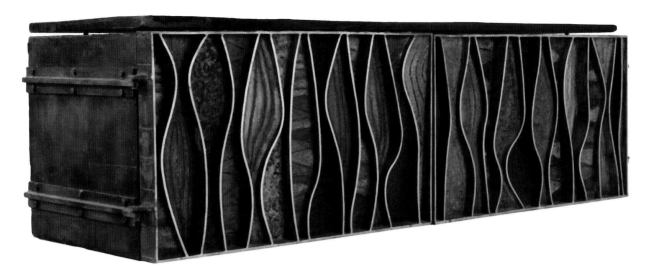

Paul Evans, wavy-front, wall-hung cabinet, patinated in vivid coloration, with natural cleft slate top, signed Paul Evans 1966, 21" x 72" x 22.5" **95,000**

Paul Evans, two-door vertical sculpture front cabinet, patinated, with edges trimmed in 23K gold-leaf, red-washed interior with three gold-leaf drawers and numerous compartments, signed Paul Evans '72, 82" x 36" x 20" **$190,000**

tables

Coffee Tables
$1,000 and under

Almost nowhere in Modernism will you find as wide a variety of expression as you will in tables. From dining tables to end tables, coffee tables, side tables, occasional tables and beyond, one of the most-used items in a household inspired the greatest names in the business to create some of their most enduring work. A keen eye and a well-developed sense of style can land you a great example, from a top name, at almost any level of price.

Coffee table, round top, rust, brown and yellow, 1960s, 30.25" x 13" **$225**

Jens Risom Design Inc. coffee table, 40" x 18" **$300**

Jens Risom (1919-)

Jens Risom is a Copenhagen-born architect who immigrated to the United States in 1939. He studied at the Copenhagen School of Arts and Crafts with Hans Wegner, where he learned the basics of the design that would make him one of the brightest stars of Modernism and one of the most successful designers of the 20th Century. He joined forces with Hans Knoll in 1941. While Knoll's original line (The Knoll 600) featured many great names, of the first 20 designs released, fully 15 were exclusive Risom. In 1946, after serving in the U.S. army under Patton, Risom struck out on his own and started his own firm, Jens Risom Design, or JRD.

Risom's designs were innovative and successful, but his true genius was in his ability to market the Risom name. His early 1950s ad campaign, "The Answer is Risom," with photographer Richard Avedon, is one of the hallmarks of 20th Century advertising. It worked so well that the company expanded in the mid-1950s to include a much bigger facility and several different furniture lines: office, hospital and library on top of the ever-popular home-furnishing lines. His original works are in the design collections of museums around the world, and Risom remains a beloved designer well into his 90s. He once summed up his philosophy of design this way: "Good design means that anything good will go well with other equally good things—contemporary or traditional. Furniture is not sculpture, nor is a particular design created only for visual appearance. Furniture should clearly satisfy all requirements: it should be used, enjoyed and respected."

Eero Saarinen, pedestal coffee table, 36" x 15" **$450**

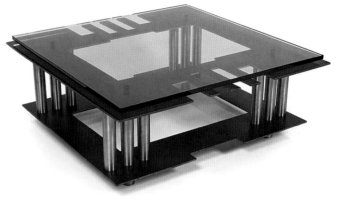

Steven Hensel, "Orpheum" coffee table, 42" sq x 17" **$475**

Coffee table in the manner of Osvaldo Borsani, 1960s, 22.5" x 24"
x 42" **$500**

Coffee table, 1960s, 43" x 14.75" **$500**

Bruno Mathsson, coffee table, 33.5" x 22.5" x 19.75" **$500**

John Mascheroni, large coffee table, 72" x 60" x 16" **$500**

Coffee table, with radiating veneer top on ebonized saber legs, 20.25" x 59" x 35.5" **$600**

Bertha Schaefer, coffee table, travertine top, 60.25" x 17" x 15" **$550**

Isamu Noguchi/Herman Miller, coffee table with three-sided plate-glass top on ebonized base, 15" x 50" x 36.5" **$550**

Knut Hesterberg, coffee table, 41.5" x 15.25" **$600**

George Nelson, La Fonda coffee table, round slate top, 30" x 17.5" **$600**

T.H. Robsjohn-Gibbings, coffee table, round walnut top 30" x 15.25" **$750**

Warren Platner, coffee table on wire base, 36" x 15" **$700**

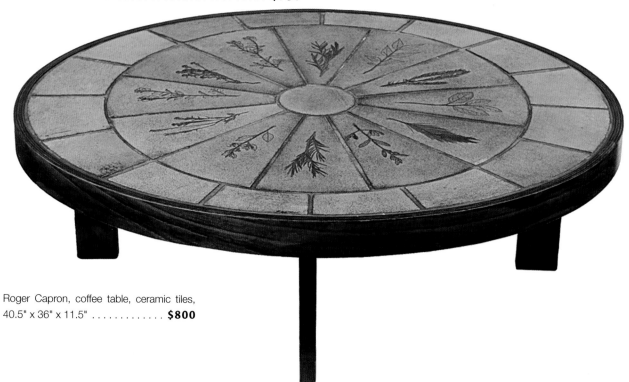

Roger Capron, coffee table, ceramic tiles, 40.5" x 36" x 11.5" **$800**

James Mont, coffee table, octagonal form, mirrored top, 65" x 18" x 16.5" **$800**

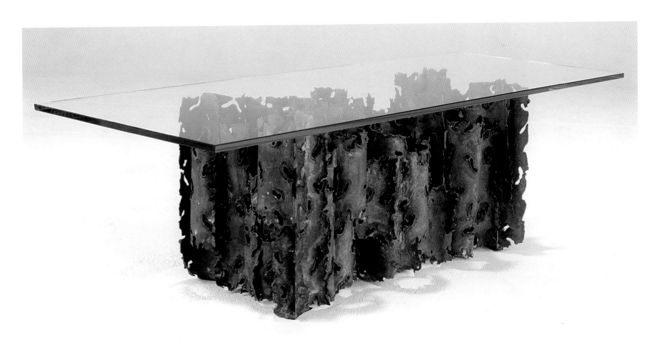

Silas Seandel, patinated and welded bronze coffee table with plate glass top, 15.5" x 51.5" x 21" **$1,000**

$1,000 to $3,000

James Mont, coffee table, Asian-inspired, 60" x 24" x 14.5" **$1,100**

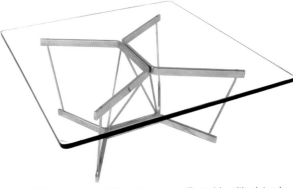

George Nelson/Herman Miller, Catenary coffee table with plate glass top on polished steel base, 15.25" x 36" sq. **$1,250**

Charles and Ray Eames, metal coffee table, 34.25" x 16.5" **$1,400**

T.H. Robsjohn-Gibbings, coffee table, elliptical top, 72.5" x 18.75" x 16" **$1,400**

Vladimir Kagan, coffee table with ebony marble top on boomerang-shaped zebrawood base, 16" x 45" x 31" **$1,500**

James Mont, coffee table with mirrored top on black lacquered base, 15.5" x 36" sq **$1,500**

Willy Rizzo, bar coffee table, stainless steel, 47.25" x 27.25" x 15" **$1,500**

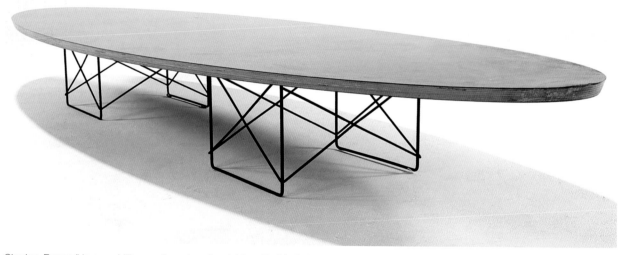

Charles Eames/Herman Miller, surfboard coffee table with black laminate top on wire base, oval Eames/Herman Miller metal tag, 10" x 89.5" x 29.5" **$1,600**

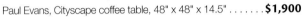

Paul Evans, Cityscape coffee table, 48" x 48" x 14.5" **$1,900**

George Nakashima / Widdicomb, walnut coffee table with inset Carpathian burled elm top, Widdicomb label, 13" x 84" x 30" **$2,000**

Edward Wormley/Dunbar, walnut and brass coffee table with polished marble extensions; open 19" x 69" x 24". **$2,000**

Edward Wormley/Dunbar, coffee table with oak veneer top on mahogany frame, Dunbar brass tag, 17" x 72" x 35" **$2,000**

Gio Ponti, "Jack" coffee table with plate glass top on ebonized wood base, 19.5" x 36". **$2,200**

Jonathon Singleton, un-flat stainless steel low coffee table, 15" x 44" x 29.5" **$2,200**

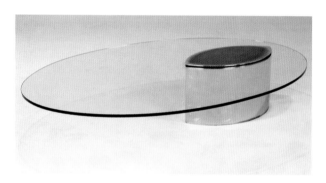

Cini Boeri, Lunaria coffee table with elliptical glass top over chromed steel base, 12.5" x 59" x 43.5" **$2,300**

Pucci De Rossi, coffee table, wenge wood top, 49" x 25" x 18" **$2,500**

Paul Laszlo, ebonized oak coffee table with inset leather top, storage compartment and painted drawer fronts, circa 1955, 21" x 54" x 35" **$2,500**

Silas Seandel, prototype coffee table with glass top on troweled stone base, 18" x 48" x 30" **$2,500**

George Nakashima / Widdicomb, coffee table with freeform top in Sundra finish, marked Widdicomb 12-6-200, 13" x 66" x 24.5".. **$2,600**

Edward Wormley, coffee table by Dunbar, open 69.5" x 24.75" x 14.5", 44" closed.................................... **$2,700**

John Keal/Brown Saltman, mahogany coffee table with biomorphic top, brown Saltman decal, 14.5" x 60" x 30".............. **$2,800**

Vladimir Kagan/Dreyfuss, walnut coffee table with plank legs supporting a tapered top, branded Kagan Dreyfuss New York—A Vladimir Kagan Design, 16" x 66" x 18.75" **$3,000**

Paul Evans, copper, bronze and pewter coffee table with inset slate top, 16" x 48" x 32"............................. **$4,250**

Willy Rizzo, travertine coffee table with steel trim, 16" x 51" x 31.5"..................................... **$3,000**

Philip and Kelvin Laverne, patinated bronze coffee table with figural engraving, signed Philip K Laverne, 16" x 48" x 36"......... **$4,750**

Robert Mapplethorpe, Geometric coffee table, 60" x 24" x 20" **$6,000**

Vladimir Kagan, tri-symmetric coffee table with biomorphic plate glass top on sculpted walnut base, 16" x 69" x 34" **$6,000**

Philip and Kelvin Laverne, patinated bronze coffee table engraved with foliate motifs, signed Philip Kelvin Laverne, 15.5" x 39" x 25" **$6,500**

James Martin, walnut coffee table with carved top, marked James Martin Woodworking New Hope, PA, 15" x 36" **$6,500**

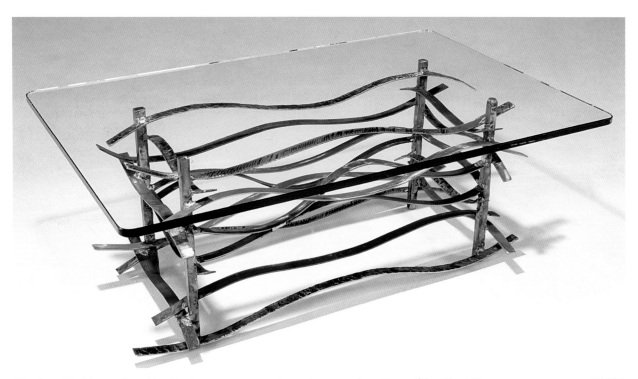

Silas Seandel, ribbon coffee table with glass top on copper, brass, bronze and steel base, 16" x 42" x 27" **$7,000**

$10,000 and up

Mira Nakashima, special redwood root burl coffee table with sled base in American black walnut, 16" x 75" x 33" **$10,000**

George Nakashima, early and rare walnut coffee table with trapezoidal top on shaped, mortised plank back and two front legs, 14.25" x 57.75" x 20" **$17,000**

Edward Wormley/Dunbar, walnut coffee table with five circular Natzler tiles covered in red glaze, brass Dunbar tag, 17.25" x 77.25" x 19.25" **$11,000**

George Nakashima, Minguren I coffee table with English oak burl top on laurel base, 1969, 17.25" x 42.5" **$60,000**

Eero Saarinen/Knoll, tulip dinette table with walnut top and two matching armchairs upholstered in red fabric, with remnant of Knoll label, table 29" x 42" . . . . **$800 set**

Gae Aulenti, Locus Solus table and four chairs, table 33" x 33" x 27", chairs 21.5" x 26" . . . . **$800 set**

Isamu Noguchi/Harry Bertoia, cyclone dining table with white laminate top on chrome base, and four Bertoia white-wire side chairs with black enameled metal bases and colored vinyl seat covers, chairs with Knoll labels, five pieces; table 29" x 48", chairs 30" x 21" x 18" **$900 set**

Patio set, round table top and three benches, 1950s, table 48" x 30", benches 41" x 16" x 17.5". . . . . **$1,200 set**

Russell Woodard, patio dining set, table and four chairs, table 48" x 29", chairs 26.5" x 23" x 30". **$1,800 set**

Eero Saarinen, pedestal dining table and four chairs, table 42" x 28.5", chairs 19.25" x 20" x 32"..................**$2,100 set**

Finn Juhl and Hvidt & Molgaard, teak gate-leg dining table by Hvidt & Molgaard, along with six adjustable cane-back dining chairs by Finn Juhl, one arm and five side, table with France & Son tag, chairs marked FD; table open 28.5" x 64" x 55.75", each sidechair 34" x 19.75" x 20"................**$2,000 set**

$3,000 to $5,000

T.H. Robsjohn-Gibbings/Widdicomb, mahogany veneer dining table on cross base, complete with one 20" leaf, together with six chairs, four side and two arm, upholstered in Chinoiserie silk fabric, table 29.5" x 57.75" x 38", armchair 34" x 23.5" x 18.5"...........**$3,250 set**

Warren Platner/Knoll, circular dining table with rosewood top on steel wire frame, and four upholstered dining chairs, Knoll Associates tags, table 28.5" x 54", chairs 30.5" x 37" x 25.5" . . . . **$5,000 set**

$5,000 to $10,000

T.H. Robsjohn-Gibbings, dining set, table and six chairs, table 48.25" x 29", chairs 21" x 21" x 37.75" . . . . **$6,000 set**

$10,000 and up

Jonathon Singleton, stainless steel dining table with broad faceted legs, and six dining chairs, metal tag, Jonathan Singleton SIG Furniture, 30" x 76.5" x 47.5" . . . . **$7,000 set**

Donald Deskey/W. & J. Sloane, 10-piece dining suite in Madrone burl veneer and Macassar ebony, extension table with six fabric-upholstered chairs and two 15" leaves, server with interior drawers and shelves, bar cabinet and china cabinet circa 1936; table (closed) 29.5" x 66" x 40", armchairs 34.5" x 23" x 20", server 36" x 66" x 20", bar 32" x 29" x 18", china cabinet 60" x 32.5" x 16" . . . . **$14,000 set**

Parzinger, drop-leaf table, harlequin pattern, closed 38.5" x 19.25" x 29", with all leaves inserted 68"......................**$225**

Parzinger, oval drop-leaf table, inset trim detail, three 14.75" leaves, closed 44.75" x 21" x 28", with leaves 94.25"............**$225**

Giancarlo Piretti, Plana table, size open 33" x 33" x 29".....**$225**

Grosfeld House table, four plumes, round glass top, 42" x 28.5" **$400**

George Nelson, gate-leg dining table, closed 40" x 18.5" x 29.75", open 64.75".....................................**$550**

Isamu Noguchi, dining table with wire base, 35.5" x 28.5"...**$750**

Drop-leaf table, Norwegian, open 58.75" x 34.75" x 29" **$850**

Eero Saarinen/Knoll, tulip dining table with white laminate top, 29" x 42" **$900**

$1,000 to $3,000

T.H. Robsjohn-Gibbings, console/dining table, abalone inlay, 68" x 19" x 29.5" **$1,000**

Dunbar, dining or hall table, round top, conical base, 37.75" x 21.25" **$1,000**

Richard Schultz/Knoll, dining or conference table, rectangular rosewood top inlaid with chrome, 29" x 36" x 76" **$1,000**

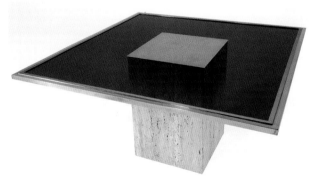

Roger Vanhevel, dining table with brass and chrome-framed smoked glass top over travertine base with etched brass center panel, signed, 27.75" x 54.75" **$1,000**

Dining table, burled wood, 1970s, 72" w x 36" d x 30" h, without leaves 42" w **$1,200**

Charlotte Perriand, dining table with pine top on black enameled steel base, 26" x 59" x 24.75" **$1,250**

Lorin Marsh, elliptical dining table covered in yellow lacquered elephant skin on brass-trimmed double-pedestal base, 29" x 108" x 48" **$1,250**

Charlotte Perriand, pine trestle table, 28" x 45" x 27.5" . . . **$1,250**

George Nelson, dining or worktable, 59" x 29.5" x 29.5" **$1,300**

Philippe Starck/Driade Aleph, dining table, M (Serie Lang),with frosted glass top on cast aluminum legs, signed, 41.5" x 60" x 14". **$1,300**

Osvaldo Borsani, dining table with radiating walnut veneer top on polished steel base, 28" x 77.75" x 47" **$1,500**

George Nakashima, walnut conoid dining table, free-edge top with two rosewood butterfly keys, 28.5" x 72" x 45" **$40,000**

George Nakashima, Frenchman's Cove rosewood dining table, single-board top with seven butterfly keys, 1981, 28.75" x 68" x 40.5" . . **$210,000**

End Tables

$1,000 to $3,000

Paul McCobb, end tables, 24" x 28" x 19.5" ....$1,300 **pair**

T.H. Robsjohn-Gibbings, end tables, 31.5" x 19.5" x 20.25" ....$1,700 **pair**

$3,000 to $5,000

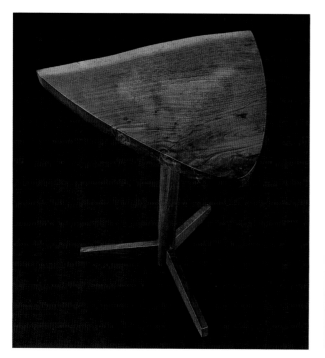

George Nakashima, walnut pedestal end table, 21.5" x 20" x 17" **$3,500**

$5,000 to $10,000

George Nakashima, walnut pedestal end table with single butterfly key to top, 21" x 28" x 28" **$7,000**

Brown Saltman, occasional tables, glass surface, 17.25" x 17.25" x 15.25" .... **$225 pair**

Jay Spectre, occasional table, wedge shaped, 15.5" x 15.5" x 18" **$125**

Peter Hvidt & Orla Molgaard, "Ax" occasional table, 43" x 19" x 22.25" **$300**

Paul Lazslo, occasional table, wedge shaped, 29.25" x 19.75" x 19.5" **$300**

Florence Knoll, occasional table, 27" x 27" x 17" **$350**

Brueton Zephyr, occasional table, 18.5" x 11 3/8" x 18" **$400**

Lacquered wood occasional tables, with brass-capped feet, 31" x 32" . . . . **$600 pair**

Occasional table, Bakelite, France, 23.75" x 18.75". **$450**

Mario Bellini, occasional/coffee tables, 35.25" x 35.25" x 15" . . . . **$700 pair**

Larry Laszlo, occasional table, black granite top, 47" x 31" x 25" **$800**

George Nakashima, occasional table, "Origins" line, boomerang shape, 30" x 30" x 21.25" **$800**

Paul Evans, occasional table base, 12" x 12" x 14" **$850**

T.H. Robsjohn-Gibbings, occasional table, 30" x 20" **$900**

Isamu Noguchi, occasional table, white laminate, birch, wire base, 23.75" x 20" **$950**

occasional tables **193**

$1,000 to $3,000

Karl Springer, occasional tables, 27" x 27" x 22.5" . . . .**$1,500 pair**

Karl Springer, rectangular wooden occasional table covered in elephant skin, along with wastebasket covered in python, table with branded leather Karl Springer Ltd. tag, table 16" x 26" x 15", wastebasket 13.25" x 8.5" sq . . . . **$1,500 both**

Eames, occasional wood coffee table, black plastic surface, 35" x 24" x 15.5" **$1,700**

Silas Seandel, bronze occasional table, biomorphic top inset with two glass panels, 17" x 25" x 21" **$3,250**

Philip & Kelvin Laverne, Ming occasional table, 23.75" x 22" **$4,000**

Paul Evans, cube occasional table covered in copper, bronze and pewter patchwork with inset slate top, 18.75" x 13" sq . . . **$4,500**

$5,000 to $10,000

Tommi Parzinger, triangular occasional tables, each 54.5" x 28" x 18", used together 40.25" sq. . . . . **$5,500 pair**

Side Tables
$1,000 and under

Greta Grossman, side table, 18" x 31.5" x 20"..........**$950**

Eero Saarinen, pedestal side table, 16" x 20.5"..........**$325**

Billy Haines/Mansic House, celadon-green glass-top side tables, Mansic House stamp, 21" x 30" x 16.5"..........**$1,000 pair**

Roger Sprunger/Dunbar, rosewood and brass side table with smoked-glass top, Dunbar metal tag, 23" x 27"........**$1,000**

Edward Wormley/Dunbar, circular side table with book-matched Persian walnut top, Dunbar brass tag, 23" x 27" **$2,000**

Vladimir Kagan, tri-symmetric side table with biomorphic plate glass top on sculpted walnut base, 19" x 31" x 24" **$2,100**

Two-tier burlwood veneer side tables on ebonized wood legs, Italy, 25" x 16.5" x 29.5" . . . . **$2,400 pair**

George Nakashima, early walnut side table with round top on four tapered, angular legs, 26" x 24" **$2,700**

$3,000 to $5,000

Vladimir Kagan, cantilevered ebonized oak side tables, their tops inset with three abstract tiles, 27" x 27.75" x 18".... **$3,500 pair**

Ico Parisi/Singer & Sons, walnut side table with book-matched top over single drawer and shelf, 25.75" x 23" x 18" **$4,500**

Tony Duquette, lacquered amoeba-shaped side tables with inset elephant skin tops, 17" x 44" x 40" .... **$4,000 pair**

Edward Wormley/Dunbar, sculpted walnut side table, its top inset with Tiffany Favrile glass tiles, Dunbar brass tag, 25" x 19.5" x 15"................................**$9,000**

Jacques Adnet, side table with a basket-shaped, stitched leather-covered top over three brass bamboo-shaped legs, under a circular glass top, 21" x 17.5"..**$10,000**

George Nakashima, side table with English walnut free-edge top on American walnut tripod base, early 1960s, 21.5" x 29" x 21" . . . **$14,000**

George Nakashima (1905-1990)

George Nakashima was often called "The Father of the American Crafts Movement," which is an appropriate appellation. His designs, resonated greatly in their day and continue to be highly in demand at auction, in shops and through George Nakashima Woodworker S.A. in New Hope, Pa. His tables – made out of huge wooden slabs with unfinished sides and joined by butterfly joints – and his Conoid chairs and benches are among the most treasured pieces in any auction, or at any show, especially if they have a provenance tying them directly back to the hand of Nakashima himself.

Nakashima, born in Spokane, Wash., was another example of the great international melding that symbolizes so much of Modern design. He was deeply influenced by his home in America's Northwest, yet the time he spent in Japan, and interred in a work camp in Idaho during World War II, were as deeply influential on his work as anything he saw or studied in his travels around the world. Nakashima was a master craftsman and woodworker, and he insisted on perfection in every step of the creation of his tables and chairs. These were not mass-produced items; they were one-of-a-kind, lovingly crafted pieces of art that doubled as furniture for those lucky enough to get one straight from the master's hand. Prices on the best original Nakashima pieces routinely reach into the high five figures.

Giotto Stoppino, stacking tables and magazine rack, 18" x 16" . . . . **$125 all**

Scandinavian nesting tables, six-sided teak tops, three, largest 21" x 14" x 20" . . . . **$150 set**

Lamp table, Donald Desky-style, round veneered wood top, 18" x 28" **$250**

Sewing table, Danish Modern, 23" x 17" x 21" **$300**

George Nelson, planter table, 19" x 30" x 26" **$325**

Console table, two-tiered form, black lacquer, 1940s, 40" x 17" x 27.25" **$700**

Walnut two-drawer side table with tray top on brass legs, 21.5" x 31" sq. **$750**

George Nelson, tray table, ash plywood, 15" x 15" x 20" **$650**

Hermann Bongaard, folding tables, 14.25" x 14.25" x 14" . . . . **$700 pair**

Eliel Saarinen, set of three nesting tables with etched-glass tops, largest 27" x 24" . . . .**$1,000 set**

Franco Campo and Carlo Graffi, cocktail table with upturned teak top on painted steel legs, branded Campo Graffi Design Home, 16" x 47" x 18" **$1,500**

Edward Wormley, nesting tables, three, largest 28" x 20" x 22" . . . . **$1,100 set**

Milo Baughman/Arch Gordon, tray table with half-moon handle in walnut, brass and enameled metal, 25" x 19" sq **$2,000**

Philippe Starck, steel console table with glass top, 16" x 47" x 18" **$2,000**

Edward Wormley, interlocking tables, black 53.5" x 23" x 24", white 85.77" x 15.5" x 15" . . . . **$2,600 pair**

Isamu Noguchi/Knoll, child's "cyclone" table no. 87, with white laminate top, black wire and birch base. Knoll Associates label, 20" x 24" **$2,700**

Edward Wormley/Dunbar, mahogany Gueridon tables with faceted posts and tripod bases, Dunbar metal tags, 28" x 22" . . . . **$2,600 pair**

$10,000 and up

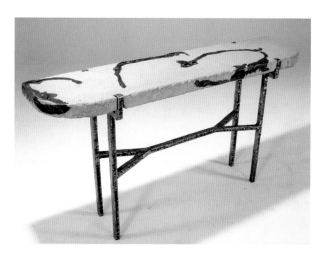

Silas Seandel, terra console table with cast stone top incised with bronze on patinated steel frame, 32" x 64" x 16" **$4,250**

Isamu Noguchi/Herman Miller, chess table with rotating, inlaid biomorphic top over cast-aluminum tray and ebonized base, 20.75" x 25" x 25" **$65,000**

accessories

Bowls, Plates

$1,000 and under

Just as the ethos and philosophy of Modernism broke open the design template of the 20th century, so, too, did it expand the places that designers could go to express themselves. In this chapter, we've assembled the best of the rest: examples of great design that didn't fit into any of the major categories of Modernism.

MS bowl, men wrestling, flaring shape, 7.25" x 2.5" **$50**

Michael and Frances Higgins, bowl, 10.25" x 4" **$75**

Ron Pruitt, fused glass plate, Chicago, 11" x 11.25" **$125**

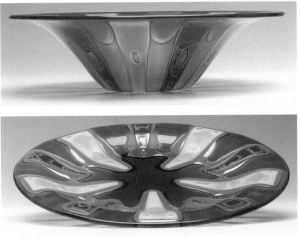

Michael and Frances Higgins, bowl and plate, each 12.25" **$150 pair**

Michael and Frances Higgins, bowls, two, larger 8.5" . . . . **$225 pair**

Rude Osolnik bowl, walnut, 10" x 2.5" **$325**

A.D. Copier, Serica glass footed bowl in iridescent yellow overlaid with burst-open crackle, acid-stamped triangular mark, 10.5" x 6.25" **$500**

Laura Andreson, bowl, circa 1972, 7" x 3" **$650**

Laura Andreson, bowl, flaring shape, 9.5" x 3" **$600**

Gertrud and Otto Natzler, bowl, orange and brown glaze, 5.5" x 2" **$1,200**

Gertrud and Otto Natzler, bowl, multi-hued blue glaze, 7" x 3" **$2,000**

Eliel Saarinen, "Contempora" bowls, set of 12, 5.5" x 1.75" **$2,600 all**

Beatrice Wood, bowl, 5.75" x 2.5" **$1,400**

Candleholders

Elsa Peretti, "Bone" candlesticks, pair, 14.25" **$350**

Walter Dorwin Teague, Knickerbocker candleholders, pair, 3.25" x 2.5" **$350**

Lino Sabattini, candlesticks with spiral arms, pair, 11.5". **$750**

Erik Hoglun/Boda Afors, 12-arm floor-standing iron candelabrum with drop crystals, and clear glass discs impressed with fish and primitive faces, 44.25" x 19.5" **$8,500**

George Nelson, table clock, orange and white body, cone base, 5.75" x 6.75" **$1,400**

George Nelson, "Pill" table clock, model 2220, 6" x 7.75" **$2,000**

George Nelson (1908-1986)

George Nelson was a force of nature; there's no denying it. He was a brilliant draftsman, a prolific and talented writer, an amazing manager of talent and a visionary designer in his own right. If his output of direct designs is not as lengthy as that of his contemporaries, it is not because he lacked vision. Nelson oversaw what is easily the most prolific and iconic period in the history of Michigan design firm Herman Miller. He oversaw names like Charles and Ray Eames, Harry Bertoia, Isamu Noguchi and Donald Knur in the post-World War II period, and the influence of that team of designers has never waned. In fact, despite the fact that Bertoia and Noguchi would both later express doubts about their involvement, the designs of that period have only increased in stature over the decades.

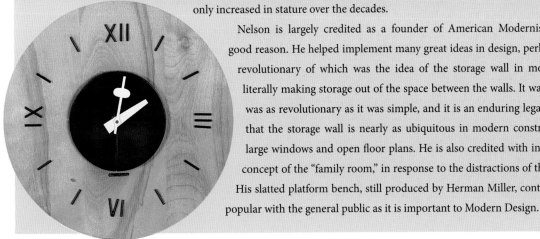

Nelson is largely credited as a founder of American Modernism, and with good reason. He helped implement many great ideas in design, perhaps the most revolutionary of which was the idea of the storage wall in modern homes, literally making storage out of the space between the walls. It was an idea that was as revolutionary as it was simple, and it is an enduring legacy to this day that the storage wall is nearly as ubiquitous in modern construction as are large windows and open floor plans. He is also credited with introducing the concept of the "family room," in response to the distractions of the atomic age. His slatted platform bench, still produced by Herman Miller, continues to be as popular with the general public as it is important to Modern Design.

George Nelson, wall clock by Howard Miller, 14" **$475**

Gilbert Rohde/Herman Miller, Model 6366 Macassar ebony table clock with chrome-plated steel details, marked Herman Miller., 6.25" x 17" x 3" **$4,750**

Gilbert Rohde/Herman Miller, Telechron burlwood veneer table clock with chrome-plated steel details, marked Herman Miller, 6" x 7.75" **$4,000**

George Nelson, "Cone" table clock, model 2218, 6.25" x 7.25" **$6,500**

George Nelson, "Clocknik" table clock, model 2270, 5" x 7" **$5,500**

Pitchers, Tea & Coffee Service

Arne Jacobsen, Cylinda Line pitcher, teapot and tray, pitcher 7.75" h, coffee pot 4.5", tray 13" . . . . **$275 set**

Deruta, pitcher and set of eight cups, pitcher 12", cups 5" . . . . **$300 set**

John Prip, Dimension tea and coffee service, tallest 8.25" . . . . **$900 set**

Planters

$1,000 and under

Robert and Paula Winokur, large raku-fired four-sided planter with two ribbon handles and four small feet, 18" x 18.5".. **$500**

Achille Castiglioni, "Albero" flower pot holder, 24" x 61"............. **$800**

$1,000 to $3,000

Architectural Supplements planter, 16" x 15.25" **$50**

Tommi Parzinger, mirrored fern holders, pair, 5" x 3" x 29" **$1,200**

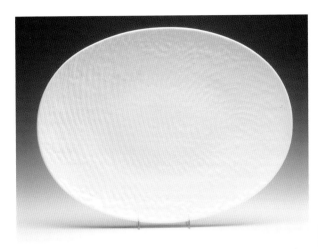

Cesar/Bernardaud, "L'Empreinte Digitale," porcelain platter after an original work, signed, titled and marked Bernardaud Limoges, 16.75" x 12" **$200**

George Nelson, China Shop trays, seven, 14" x 18" . . . **$275 set**

Karl Springer, travertine mosaic trays, Karl Springer tags, set of four, each 14" . . . . **$1,000 set**

Radios

Zanuso & Sapper, "TS 502" radios, black, white and orange, three, each 8.75" x 5" x 5". . . . . **$600 all**

Isamu Noguchi/Zenith, Bakelite radio nurse, embossed marks **$6,000**

Rugs, Textiles

Rug, wool, Modern geometric designs, 48.5" x 68.5" **$225**

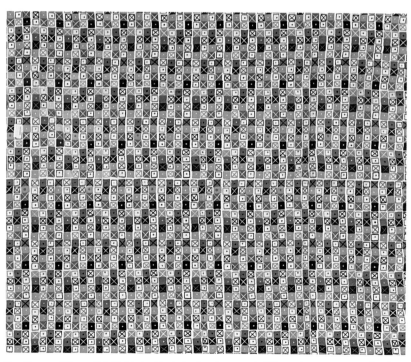

Ray Eames, "Cross Patch" fabric, black, teal and mustard, 50" x 54" **$2,600**

Orrefors vase, green glass, 9.75" . . . **$100**

Raymor, vase and bowl, vase 17.5", bowl 6" x 5" . . . .**$225 both**

Heikki Orvola, vase for Nuutajärvi Notsjö, 12". **$325**

Medina Art Glass vase, Malta, 4.25" x 6.5" **$125**

Eugene Deutch, vase, brown drip glaze, 5.5" **$175**

Eugene Deutch, vase, disc-shaped form, 7" x 5.5" **$350**

Timo Sarpaneva, "Orchid" vase, clear glass, 3" x 10.5" **$350**

Vases by Holmegaard, Denmark, three, tallest 17" . . . . **$350 all**

Floris Meydam/Leerdam, pillow vase of orange and white striped glass, marked Leerdam, 6.75" x 9.25" **$750**

Gambone, vase, ivory matt glaze, painted lines at bottom, 2.25" x 10.5" **$425**

Polia Pillin vases with designs of birds, people and fish, three, tallest 6" . . . . **$550 all**

Tapio Wirkkala, silver vase on teak base, signed TW with hallmarks, 10.5"............................... **$650**

Barbini, fazzoletto clear glass vase with white striations, signed, 15" x 14".......................................**$950**

Polia Pillin, vase with designs of figures and horses, 7" x 8.5".......................................**$850**

Paolo Venini/Venini, stoppered bottle of blue incalmo glass with red mezza filigrana center, circular mark, Venini Murano, 7" x 8.5".................................. **$900**

$1,000 to $3,000

Beatrice Wood, vase, gourd shape, 4" x 9"......................**$1,200**

Laura Andreson, vase, purple and gray metallic glaze, 2.5" x 3".........**$1,300**

Beatrice Wood, vase, 3.5" x 6.5" ... **$1,400**

Fulvio Bianconi/Venini, corseted "fasce verticale" glass vase in orange and green, etched three-line mark Venini Murano Italia, 12.5" x 3.5"..................**$1,250**

Venini, Tessuto glass vase with cupped rim, three-line stamp Venini Murano Italy, 8.5" x 3.5"...................**$1,600**

Fulvio Bianconi/Venini, bottle-shaped blown glass vase in green with broad red bands, etched three-line mark Venini Murano Italia, 14.5" x 3.5"..................**$1,500**

Toni Zucherri/Venini, Crepuscolo lavender glass vase with blue insert, mid-1960s, marked with three-line Venini Murano Italia acid stamp, 12" x 10".........**$1,600**

Livio Seguso/Pauly, Lattimo glass vase with asymmetrical rim and amber center, marked Des. L. Seguso Pauly, 12.25" x 9" ...**$2,500**

Gertrud & Otto Natzler, vase, tan glaze under a green drip glaze, 8.5" **$5,500**

Thomas Stearns, "Spirolato" vase, 4" x 11" **$8,500**

Fulvio Bianconi, "pezzato" vase, for Venini, 7.5" x 8" **$9,500**

Other Objects

Laura Andreson, ceramic covered box, rounded, 4.5" x 2" **$450**

Bucket, Modern round form, Danish, 17.5" x 16" **$125**

Edward Wormley, globe and stand, 21" x 36" **$900**

Mathieu Mategot-style wastebasket, 10" x 15" **$475**

Paul Evans /Phillip Lloyd Powell, steel and bronze bell with walnut handle, 11.5" x 2.25". **$2,600**

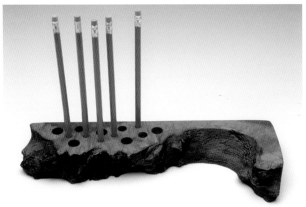

George Nakashima, burlwood pencil holder, circa 1969, 1.75" x 13" x 4.5" **$3,000**

Peter Voulkos, thrown stoneware ice bucket with torn rim and gouged surface, anagama fired and covered in bronze and brown glazes, signed on bottom VOULKOS 79, 8.5" x 10". **$20,000**

Wharton Esherick, sculpted cherry library ladder with dovetailed construction on twisted post, 52.5" x 17" x 17". **$42,500**

art

Catalogs, Drawings, Lithographs, Paintings, Posters, Prints

$1,000 and under

There is such a wide variety of art and artists in the "Modern" realm that the subject deserves a price guide all by itself. The category contains many of the most well-known names in art, and ranges from literal interpretations to the wholly abstract.

Robert A. Eckert, architectural papers in trunk with original and reproduced drawings and blueprints **$325**

Stephen Frykholm, Fruit Salad Annual Summer Picnic poster, 39.5" x 25" **$100**

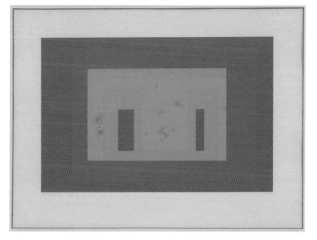

Josef Albers, Variant I, 1966; Screen print in colors (framed); signed, dated, titled and numbered 93/200, 8.5" x 13.25" (image), 12" x 16.5" (sheet) **$400**

Andy Warhol, two books and puzzle . . . . **$400 all**

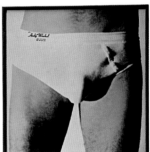

Andy Warhol, framed album covers, nine. . . . . **$800 all**

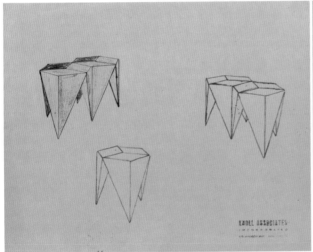
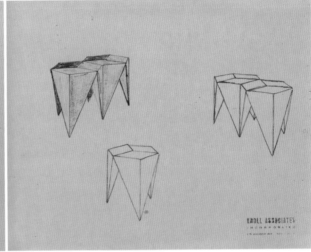

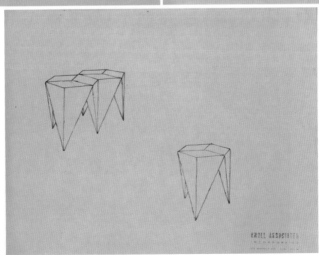

Isamu Noguchi/Knoll, three lithographs illustrating Noguchi's overall concept for an exotic sculptured table. Each stamped Knoll Associates/Incorporated/575 Madison Ave. New York NY., each lithograph: 8.5" x 11" . . . . **$800 all**

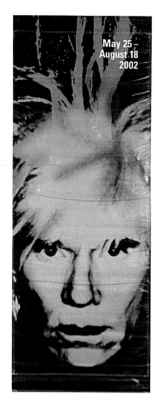

Andy Warhol, "Andy" exhibition banner, 35" x 95" **$800**

Stanley Twardowicz, Untitled, 1984, acrylic on paper (framed), signed and dated, 22.4" x 17" **$1,000**

Philip and Kelvin Laverne, acid-etched and patinated metal panel depicting horses, 23.75" x 27.75" **$900**

Paper dress, Universal Studios, circa 1968, silkscreen, 37.5" long **$1,000**

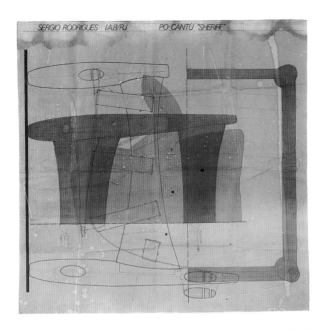

Sergio Rodrigues, design for Sheriff chair, framed under glass. Sight: 39" x 40" **$1,500**

Rolph Scarlett, Untitled, watercolor on paper (framed); signed; 11" x 15" **$1,600**

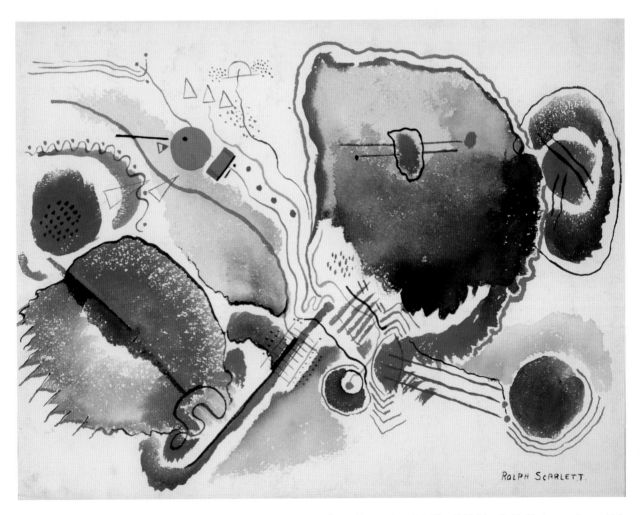

Rolph Scarlett, two works of art: Untitled; gouache and ink on paper, pictured here; signed; 9.8" x 13.5" (sheet); Untitled; gouache and ink on paper (framed); Signed **$1,600**

catalogs, drawings, lithographs, paintings, posters, prints **233**

Josef Albers, White Line Squares X, 1966; Screen print in colors (framed); signed, dated, titled and numbered 33/125. 16" x 16" **$2,200**

Norman Carton, Tempo, circa 1950s, oil on canvas, signed, 64" x 51.25" **$3,000**

Rex Ashlock, Dark Red on Orange with Moon, oil on canvas; dated with stamped signature and estate stamp; 1960, 80" x 70" **$3,000**

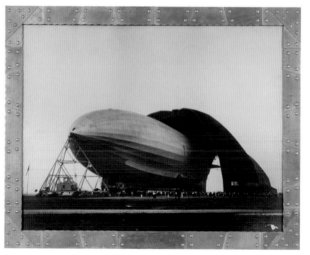

Margaret Bourke-White, United States Airship "Akron," 1931, gelatin silver print (framed), signed, 17.25" x 22.75" (sight), 20.25" x 26" (with frame) **$2,000**

Dorothy Morang, Conclave, 1947, oil on Masonite (framed); signed and dated, 22" x 30" **$4,500**

Richard Hambleton, Untitled (Shadow Man), acrylic on canvas, 70.5" x 46" **$4,750**

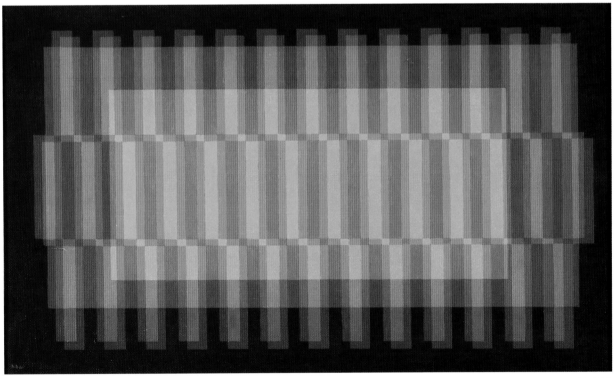

Hannes Beckmann, Facade, 1961, oil on Masonite; signed, dated and titled, 18" x 30" **$3,250**

$5,000 to $10,000

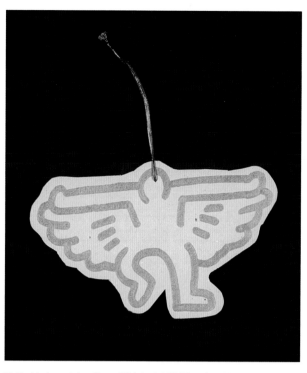

Keith Haring, Untitled, 1989, screen print in colors (framed), signed; from an edition of 60; 8" x 8", publisher: Martin Lawrence Limited Editions Inc., New York **$8,500**

Keith Haring, John (from Night of 100 Trees), 1989, gold enamel on cardboard (framed); Signed, dated and titled, publisher: Martin Lawrence Limited Editions Inc., New York, 7.5" x 12" **$8,000**

Boris Lovet-Lorski, Cosmism, 1960, oil on canvas, framed, signed, dated and titled, 50" x 42" **$6,500**

Richard Hambleton, Untitled, gold leaf on paper (framed), signed, 40" x 34" (sheet) **$7,500**

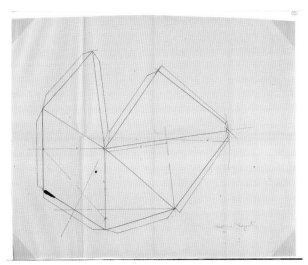

Isamu Noguchi/Knoll, pencil and ink blueprint drawings for Knoll, each signed Isamu Noguchi in pencil, set of nine, 28" x 36" and 32" x 40". **$14,000**

Norman Carton, Blue Night, 1950s; oil on canvas; signed, 84" x 64". **$13,000**

Robert Morris, Untitled, 1983-84, hydrocal and pastel on paper (inset in metal trays), 57.25" x 71.5". **$16,000**

Sculpture
$1,000 and under

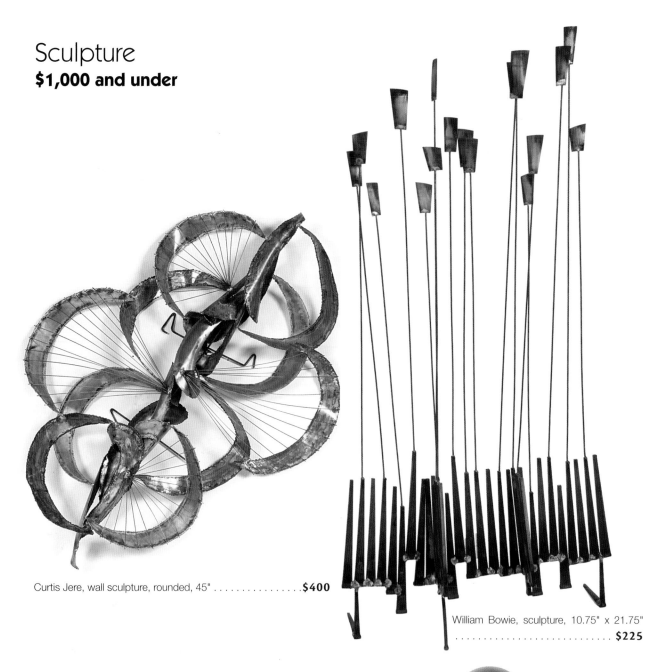

Curtis Jere, wall sculpture, rounded, 45" **$400**

William Bowie, sculpture, 10.75" x 21.75"
. . . . **$225**

Carmelo Cappello, "Forma Orizzontale Circolare," 13.5", with an Alessi "Narciso" sculpture, 8.5" x 6.5" x 6" . . . . **$250 both**

Harris Strong, framed tiles, each 10" x 10" . . . . **$400 pair**

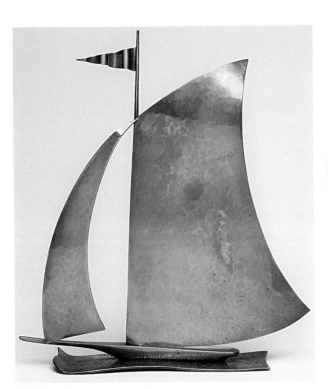

Hagenauer, boat sculpture, brass, 10.25" x 2" x 11.25" **$400**

Weber Costello, Black Ocean globe, 12" x 16" **$425**

Irving Poole, sculpture, with clay pegs, 15" x 5.5" **$500**

Russell Secrest, sculpture, no. 9/100, 17.75" **$500**

A. Hovisaari/Arabia, Glazed porcelain plaque by AA Hovisaari, 1967. Signed and dated 3-67, Finland, 14.75" x 11.5"...... **$600**

Harris Strong, tile mosaic, 15 tiles, framed size: 24" x 36" **$500**

Curtis Jeré, wall sculpture, geometric, 59" x 5" x 27"..**$950**

Dennis Jones, sculpture "Opposed Tension," circa 1990, overall 14.5" x 10.25" x 50".............................**$950**

Jeff Koons, skateboard deck, blue, 31" x 8"...........**$1,000**

Stephen Montgomery, glazed terra cotta sculpture, "Untitled #3," 1977, signed Montgomery, 39.75" x 13.75"............**$1,100**

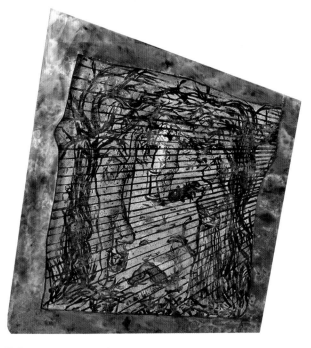

Philip and Kelvin Laverne, asymmetrical plaque in sculpted bronze and pewter with enamels, signed Philip K. Laverne, with label from Seymour Gallery, Ltd., New York, 40" x 32.5".........**$1,200**

Stephen Montgomery, monolithic painted ceramic sculpture, 1978, signed S.M. 78, 60" x 8" x 5.5"...................**$1,100**

Dennis Byng, Three works of art: Untitled, 1967, signed and dated, 11.5" high; Golash, 1974, Lucite and stone, dated and titled, Untitled, 1984, Lucite; signed and dated . . . . **$1,500 all**

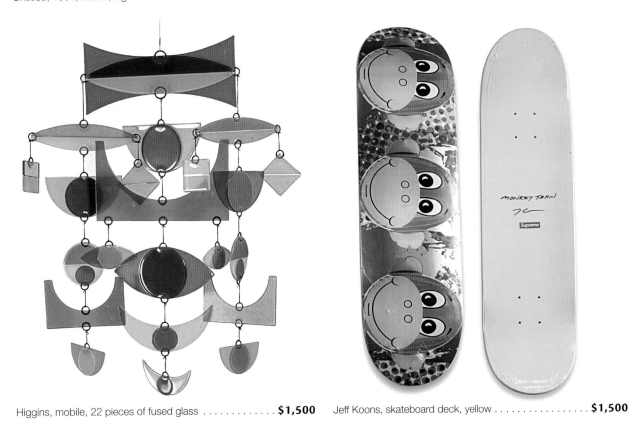

Higgins, mobile, 22 pieces of fused glass . . . . **$1,500**   Jeff Koons, skateboard deck, yellow **$1,500**

Philip and Kelvin Laverne, plaque, "Woman with Basket of Fruit," in hand-sculpted bronze, pewter and enamels, signed Philip K. Laverne, with label from Seymour Gallery, Ltd., New York, 36" x 23.5"................................. **$1,500**

Howard Kottler, glazed earthenware sculptural vessel, "Lemon Punch Pot," signed Kottler........................ **$1,700**

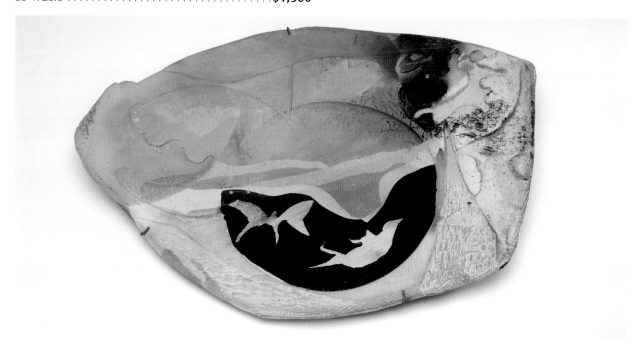

Paul Soldner, stoneware wall-hanging sculpture, "Helios Lumes," 1979, 24.5" x 17"...................................... **$1,700**

Kazuo Kadonga, carved Keyaki wood sculpture, "Sacred Wood", 6" x 24" x 4.5" **$1,800**

Studio Simon, Omaggio ad Andy Warhol, silkscreen printed on recycled paint drum topped with white velveteen cushion, marked A Omagoio Warhol Ultramobile Simon, Bologna Italy, 17.5" x 12" **$2,600**

Stephen Montgomery, monumental columnar ceramic sculpture, Octagonist, 1979 . . . . **$2,000**

Jun Kaneko, large glazed ceramic wall-hanging sculpture, 1979, signed and dated, 4" x 24.5" **$4,000**

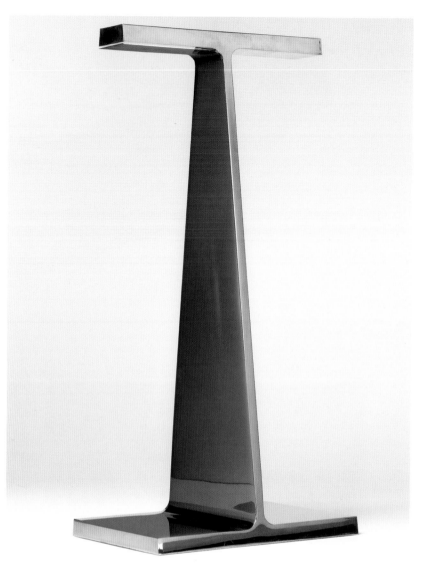

James Prestini, Number 327, 1950, Nickel plated steel, signed and titled, 24.5" x 11.8" x 8" **$4,250**

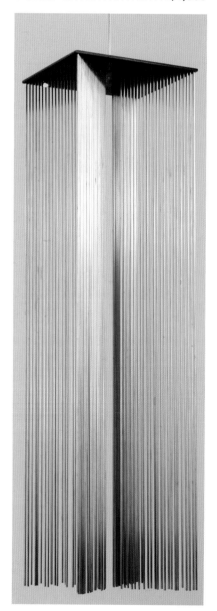

Klaus Ihlenfeld, Untitled, 1970s, stainless steel, 47.25" long (including hanging element) **$4,000**

Jun Kaneko, large glazed ceramic charger, 1983, signed and dated., 3.5" x 25" . . . **$4,500**

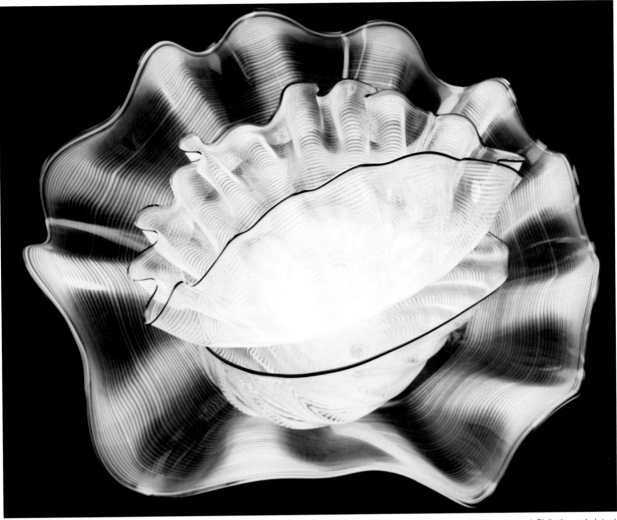

Dale Chihuly, three-piece Seaform set in clear glass with opalescent swirls and black lip wraps, largest piece engraved Chihuly and dated 1984, 7.5" x 18.5" **$9,000**

$10,000 and up

Ralph Bacerra, glazed ceramic sculpture on stand, one of 10 in the Animal series, 1976, 35" x 38" **$11,000**

Claire Falkenstein, welded copper and fused glass sculpture, 1975, signed and dated, 15" x 22" **$13,000**

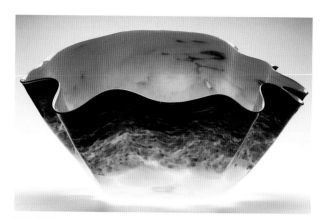

Dale Chihuly, large macchia of cobalt, vermilion and white mottled glass, acid-etched signature and date, 16" x 31"......**$14,000**

Harry Bertoia (1915-1978)

It's hard to say whether Harry Bertoia is best-known today for his amazing furniture design as part of the main group of designers that came out of the Cranbrook Academy, or as an artist and sculptor whose major works command hundreds of thousands of dollars at auction today. Bertoia's early work as a furniture designer was done with the Evans Furniture Co. in California, in the company of the Eameses as well as Eero Saarinen. Between the Eameses, Saarinen and Bertoia, the process of molding plywood would be perfected and eventually applied to furniture design. In 1950 Bertoia moved to Knoll and began the furniture work that would free him up financially to focus exclusively on his artwork.

The piece of furniture that would set Bertoia free was the Diamond Chair. It bore all the hallmarks that would become associated with his sculpture: Lots of wire, lots of open space, impeccable balance. It was an immediate success, hailed rightly as a masterpiece of design. It was not too long before he applied his philosophies to art and that art began making Bertoia not only fabulously rich, but also world-famous. His wire creations are in the permanent collections of museums all over the planet. To get one at auction, of any size, can potentially cost a buyer tens of thousands of dollars. Original versions of his furniture, specifically the Diamond Chair, are also hard to come by and are priced accordingly. The good news, though, is that the chair is still in production and you can pick up a newer one any number of venues.

Harry Bertoia, Split Spray, 1966, 40" high **$14,000**

Pablo Picasso/Egidio Constantini, "Donna Seduta", blue corroso glass sculpture of a seated woman, executed for La Fucina Degli Angeli (The Forge of Angels), inscribed P. Picasso/E. Costantini/Fucina Angeli/Venesia/P-A/1954, with copyright, 18" **$15,000**

Harry Bertoia, Untitled (Sonambient), 1965, gold-plated stainless steel on brass base, 25" high (including base) **$16,000**

Harry Bertoia, Pine Tree, 1966; stainless steel, 71.75" high (with base). . . . **$50,000**

Harry Bertoia, Willow, stainless steel, 66" high. **$37,500**

Isamu Noguchi/Gemini G.E.L., Neo-Lithic, hot-dipped galvanized steel sculpture, welded initials and date (i.n. 82.), 1983, 72" x 26.5" x 16.5" **$75,000**

Isamu Noguchi/G.E.L., galvanized steel sculpture, "Wind Catcher," embossed I.N. 82. Label: Isamu Noguchi, Wind Catcher 6/18 Gemini G.E.L. Isamu Noguchi 1983, 121" x 17.25" x 17.5" **$80,000**

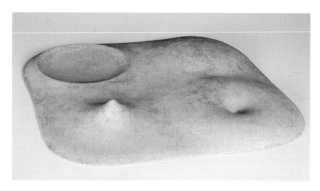

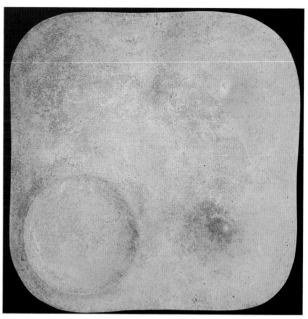

Isamu Noguchi, magnesite sculptural relief, possibly a maquette for a playground design, incised IN on back, 1940s, 16.5" x 16.5" **$180,000**

Textile Art
$1,000 and under

Harris Strong, wall hanging, 36" x 9" **$150**

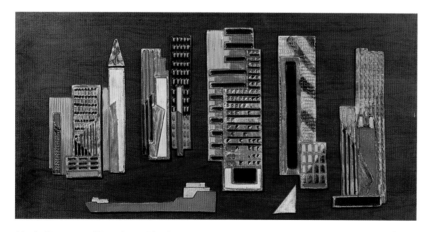

Harris Strong, wall hanging, 48" x 24" **$250**

Harris Strong, wall hanging, 11" x 36" **$325**

Verner Panton, "Geometri" rug/tapestry, 62" x 93" **$550**

Tapestry, 1950s, 75" x 45" **$500**

Alexander Smith after Henri Matisse, hand woven wool carpet, "Mimosa," woven initial HM, 56.5" x 36" **$1,000**

$1,000 to $3,000

Andy Warhol, The Souper Dress, screenprint in colors on cotton paper dress, circa 1965, titled on original label at collar, with care instructions, 38" long. **$2,000**

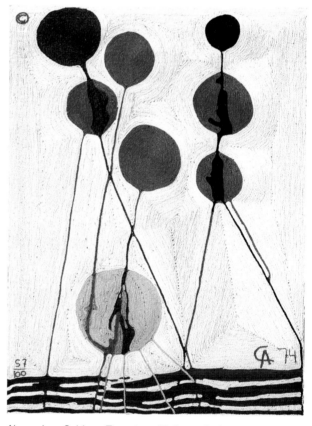

Alexander Calder, Tapestry, "Balloons," in Maguey fiber with abstract design in navy, yellow, red, peach and black, 1974, Bon Art tag, signed with embroidered copyright, CA 74 57/100, 6' x 8' **$4,500**

index

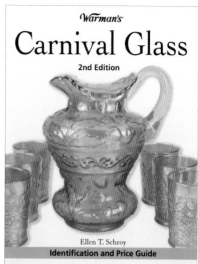

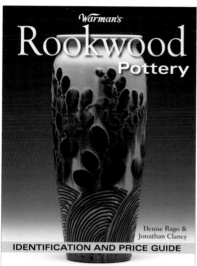
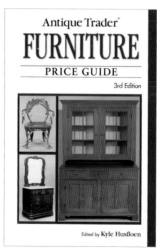
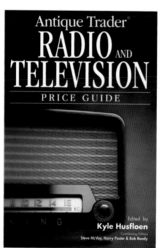